Knitting
Through It

Knitting Through It

Through It

INSPIRING STORIES
for Times *of* Trouble

Lela Nargi, Editor

Voyageur Press

First published in 2008 by Voyageur Press, an imprint of MBI
Publishing Company LLC, Galtier Plaza, Suite 200, 380 Jackson Street,
St. Paul, MN 55101 USA

Voyageur Press titles are also available at discounts in bulk quantity for
industrial or sales-promotional use. For details write to Special Sales
Manager at MBI Publishing Company, Galtier Plaza, Suite 200, 380
Jackson Street, St. Paul, MN 55101 USA.

To find out more about our books, join us online at
www.voyageurpress.com.

ISBN-13: 978-0-7603-3005-0

Editor: Kari Cornell   Designer: Sara Holle
Printed in the United States of America

Library of Congress Cataloging-in-Publication Data
Knitting through it : inspiring stories for times of trouble / Lela
Nargi, editor.
     p. cm.
 ISBN 978-0-7603-3005-0 (plc w/ jacket)
 1. Knitting. 2. Knitting—Anecdotes. 3. Knitters (Persons)—United
States. I. Nargi, Lela.
TT820.K723 2008
746.43'2—dc22   2007030875

For Rob &
For Ada, as ever

Contents

... Families in Motion

... Relationships

Introduction

B efore I started to write books, I was a journalist for fifteen years. My love for the profession had nothing at all to do with a Woodward-and-Bernstein drive to unearth politics' Big Story; with a veteran war correspondent's itch to find the world's hot spots; or with a gossip columnist's fascination with celebrity. Rather, I was drawn, always, to stories about so-called "regular" people, and the small details of their lives seemed to tell me so much about what was relevant and poignant in the way that we all go about living our lives, every day. I liked the process of tracking down people with stories to tell and, most of all, I liked sitting in a room with them and listening to them talk.

This proclivity of mine for the small story did not disappear when I left journalism. It infuses the books that I write and compile now. It began with *Knitting Lessons: Tales from the Knitting Path* (Tarcher/Penguin 2001), in which I interviewed knitters around the country in order to attempt at least marginally to answer the question: "Who knits, and why?" And it continues with the volume you now hold in your hands.

This collection was born from the vaguest research pursuit. One idle morning, as I sat browsing the Internet, I stumbled upon the Library of Congress's American Memory project—a vast collection of every sort of picture and document pertaining to the American experience. Needing a word to plug into the search engine so that I could test the site and its scope, I typed "knitting," and up came several hundred photographs, letters, newspaper articles, records, and reports, all including some reference to knitting. Most compelling were the photographs of myriad and varied knitters—some of them rare and their subjects wholly unexpected—spanning almost 200 years. There were certain life histories drawn up under the auspices of the Works Progress Administration (WPA), which were so vividly constructed that to read them was like sitting in a room and listening to fascinating people reminisce. Considered together, the photos, these histories, and a number of other, odd-ball papers, created a new template against which to contemplate the question: "Who knits, and why?"

Many people are at least aware of the WPA's Federal Writers' Project. During the Great Depression of the 1930s, the United States government hired some 6,500 unemployed writers to, among other things, compile a "documentary" of narratives and lore that would "be used as the basis for anthologies which would form a composite and comprehensive portrait of various groups of people in America," according to the Library of Congress. Working throughout the decade, the writers, some of them working under the narrower umbrella of the Folklore Project, collected almost 10,000 "life stories" from men and women, rural and urban, old and young, black and white. As Ann Banks notes in her book *First Person America*, many of these Americans "remembered the nineteenth century as vividly as some people now recall the Depression years." Their words, documented straight, verbatim, or curled around accompanying text by their interviewers, are often lyrical, poignant, and rich with information and imagery. Included in this collection are a number of historical excerpts that go a long way toward showing who ordinary knitters were, not just in the early half of the twentieth century, but back to immigrant landings on this soil. When read in conjunction with contemporary essays by Donna Druchunas, Sherri Wood, and eleven other knitters of today, they also show that who we were is who we are.

As for *why* we knit, this collection aims to illustrate only one of the *whys*—to see us through adversity of one fashion or another. Some of the subjects of the life histories knit as they recite litanies of hardship; others speak of their mothers and sisters and grandmothers knitting; still others— the majority—tell of their own experience with knitting in times of strife, either as a means to make money or as a way to give hands that were accustomed to working something to do. In some instances, adversity is as deep and resonant as a prison term (Sherri Wood's "1,200 Hats: Art and Healing in the Making"); in others, it revolves around the more personal and subjective ("Knitting Through Red States vs. Blue States" by Erica Pearson; "Knitting: My Urban Escape" by Barbara DeMarco-Barrett). In one instance—Donna Druchunas's "Knitting Softens the Impact as Worlds Collide"—it picks up a current thread in a long history of hardship and poverty among Native Americans that began, it can be argued, with European arrivals here. And always, it is about relationships: with friends and husbands, the world at large, and ourselves.

It is my hope that this book will not be seen to attempt to provide a definitive conclusion on *Knitting Through It*, but that it will lead to further thought and discussion of the subject—and for anyone who has ever knit through it themselves, it can offer a glimmer of hope.

Knitting Through... Charity

Weaving the Past into the Future
by Christy Breedlove

"Oh, yeah," I thought as I raced up a hill on my bicycle. "Eat my dust, Lance Armstrong." I laughed evilly. No one could catch me as I raced down the hill. No one, except a two-inch stick. I saw it just in time to flip over my bike and land on the hot asphalt. I was pretty sure the bike was okay. After all, I'd cushioned its fall with my body; my left arm was not so lucky.

Twenty-four hours and one marathon surgery later, I was ensconced in my bed with a makeshift cast. My wrist was smashed into forty pieces, and my elbow was broken in three places. The surgeon said even he got sick when he looked at my X-ray. He had reattached my elbow using wires, and my wrist was held together with a plate and more wire. The physical therapy would be long.

After the surgery, my wrist stiffened up like an indignant Southerner meeting a new Yankee neighbor. The physical therapist suggested weight lifting as a way to keep it supple. I nixed that idea. In my experience, weights can move on their own and end up on my floor, right in front of the bathroom door in the middle of the night. Insidious little weasels, they lie in wait (pun intended) for the unsuspecting toe. Not to be deterred by my protests, the therapist thoughtlessly left me with a pair of ten-pound weights. She also suggested that knitting might loosen my wrist so that arthritis would not set in.

Immediately, I recalled my initial experience with knitting needles three years earlier. My first project was still hidden deep in my closet. Stitched clumsily together, the cheap ivory yarn was supposed to be my first scarf, but instead it resembled a trapezoid that had squeaked in protest at my tight knitting. Now it was gathering dust with a craft book and some handwritten instructions and abbreviations that I could not understand. The writing and the knitting steps had long faded, but I clearly remembered my first knitting teacher.

I was working at a family violence shelter as a social worker when I made that disastrous ivory scarf. Every day at the shelter brought new emergencies. This victim needed counseling, money, and shoes. Another needed an emergency temporary restraining order. Yet another was detoxing from a meth addiction. Despite all the myriad of ongoing problems, the small staff persevered. The shelter tapped large businesses and foundations for money. Donations that were both financial and in-kind—second-hand clothes, soap, toothpaste, appliances, and other necessities—poured in at an astonishing rate. Amid this maelstrom, one lonely cardboard box stood out and still stands out in my memory.

A note accompanied it. Ava, a retired lady on a fixed income, wanted to help in her small way and she wanted to make a difference. The box she had sent was filled with lovingly made, hand-knit scarves and hats. They weren't fancy, nor would they keep the shelter afloat, but they would keep a few souls alive. Here, a lone knitter was reaching out and trying to improve the world one small garment at a time. One of Ava's scarves would warm the neck of a child who was fleeing from his home without even a pair of socks. Her simple beanie would block the winter wind for a single mother walking home to her children after work. Her gifts would remind these victims that there are people in this world who care for others and that love, not violence, is the norm.

Social work is a demanding master. To paraphrase an old quote, there's no one to counsel the counselor. Soon after Ava's gift arrived, I reached an all-time high on the stress-o-meter and was fast approaching apathy—a horrible thing to happen to someone in my field, where empathy is critical. My husband was increasingly concerned about my negative state of mind. He suggested that I take up a hobby. The next month, Santa left an archery set under the tree—brave of Santa, since my body is riddled with scars from previous, klutzy encounters with hobbies. One scar on my leg resulted from an encounter with a hot carburetor on a motorbike. A hot glue gun and a pair of scissors used during a scrapbooking class left behind two more scars on my arm.

When an ADT sign in our front yard died from one of my arrow's puncture wounds, my husband went in search of a safe hobby for me. He reminded me that his grandmother once offered to teach me knitting after I'd admired the baby blanket she made for my son. I made arrangements to begin lessons with her, but sadly Grandmama broke her hip and eventually had to move to an assisted living facility that was two hours away from us. I racked my brain for someone who could help. Finances were extremely tight in our house at the time, so a private class at a craft store was out of the question.

I recalled the exquisite scarves from Ava. Though I'd never met her, I called and asked her advice about where I could learn to knit inexpensively. She was hesitant and perhaps a bit unnerved by my proclaimed interest in knitting, but she bravely offered to teach me herself. I told her about my lack of a craft gene and reiterated my limited financial circumstances. She said she would not charge to teach a friend to knit. Her only caveat was that I come to her home: She didn't drive because of her failing eyesight—not surprising since she was nearing eighty years old.

I arrived for my visit with Ava to find her lawn was immaculate and her home even more so. Southern dowager came to mind when I met her. Her bluish hair was piled high in a bun, her green eyes peered over her Jackie O–style glasses, and a large square diamond graced her left ring finger. But her gnarled fingers were also crippled with arthritis; her paper-thin skin stretched tautly across hands that were dotted with brown age spots. She was stooped over with age and attired in a pink dress from the 1950s; nonetheless, she commanded respect.

Ava had years of experience to impart, but her children were not interested in her past. Her daughter worked full-time, and her grandchildren were away at college. They were too cool for their grandmother, who lived in the sticks and had never advanced past high school. But when it came to knitting and life, I found Ava was wiser than any college professor I knew.

After dispensing with her hostess duties by bringing me a glass of sweet tea, Ava motioned for me to sit on a chair in her dining room, which she had converted to a craft room. Ava was a long-time quilter, but she had also branched out into other areas of fiber art—crochet, needlework, and knitting. She was a veritable one-woman Hobby Lobby. In short, she was my complete opposite.

Watching her knit was like watching a wizard weaving a spell as she moved yarn at the speed of light from one needle to another. A true teacher, she saw how I struggled with coordination and didn't laugh at me. Instead, in simple terms, she described the how-to's of knitting for a complete craft moron.

"In, twist, scoop, off," she chanted in the rhythm of an old square dance caller. "Up and in. Twist to the front. Scoop like ice cream. Off the slide."

I didn't realize I was biting my tongue until I yelled in triumph at my first completed stitch and drew blood. I quickly followed her chant—this time calling upon my Catholic background and adding a Gregorian slant to it.

Minutes clicked by, and I finally finished my first row of ten stitches. I started the next row but soon made mistakes. I wrapped my yarn three times around the needle, dropped one stitch, accidentally purled, knit under two stitches, and generally screwed up the second row. I heaved a sigh of frustration and jutted my lip out like a two-year-old child. Ava patiently put down her project, repaired mine, and returned to hers. She kept a running commentary on her philosophies, while her metal needles clicked like a Morse code.

While growing up during the Great Depression, Ava learned from her mother not to waste anything. This frugalness led to a lifelong devotion to quilting from scraps and sewing clothes from old feedbags. Her mother also taught her crochet and knitting. Ava proudly stated that she hadn't bought any of her clothes ready made until she purchased her wedding gown second-hand from a friend.

Ava also described how her mother was always the one who showed up at a neighbor's house to bring food and comfort when a relative had died. Like her mother, Ava opted to serve behind the scenes through her church and her children's schools rather than adopting a more radical approach to bettering her community. She learned from her mother that change starts to happen when one person simply helps a neighbor in need.

I was so engrossed in my work that I didn't notice Ava had stopped knitting and started to discretely rub her knuckles.

"Arthritis," she said when I finally looked over. "It flares up after awhile." She motioned to the sapphire blue scarf she was knitting. When I had arrived at her dining table, it had only been two inches long; now it resembled one of the beautiful scarves I had seen at Nordstrom's priced at $75.00. Thick and lush, the scarf draped gracefully over the table; it was knit in an intricate pattern that I didn't recognize.

"I've got to add fringe."

"What kind of yarn is this?" I couldn't resist touching it. Even as an inexperienced knitter, I could feel the quality of the soft fabric.

"It's 100 percent alpaca," Ava said, almost reverently. "It costs around $20 a skein."

"Wow." I drew a breath and held it, not wanting to breathe on the scarf in the off chance this might unravel it. "Your daughter will love this."

"My daughter?" Ava narrowed her piercing green eyes. "This is going to the shelter."

And with that brief statement, I finally understood charity. Oh, I knew what it meant and occasionally practiced it myself. But Ava was a different story. Here was an elderly woman on a fixed income spending $20 on a pure alpaca skein. (Although I could not yet tell the difference between alpaca and aardvark, I knew alpaca was special.) As if the expense of the yarn wasn't enough, Ava knit through considerable pain to create a work of art for a wounded person she had never met. Then she did it again and again.

That day, I left two hours later and a little wiser. Unfortunately, as is the way with mothers, I became very busy and soon forgot Ava's knitting lesson and the cheap ivory scarf. But I didn't forget her matter-of-fact advice about the true spirit of giving.

A year later, I had quit working at the shelter to stay home with my two children, and I heard third-hand of Ava's death two weeks after it happened. I had missed her funeral, but I wondered if I even would have been welcome. After all, I had only met Ava once and spent a mere two hours in her company. Would her daughter understand how Ava impacted my life? Thanks to Ava and her shining example, quietly and without fanfare, I started doing little things to change the world for the better—picking up someone else's litter, volunteering at a rape crisis center, donating blood, and acting as a Big Sister to a child. I also charged my children with the same challenge Ava had placed before me.

Three years later, as the sun shone through the physical therapist's exercise room, I vowed to recapture the knitting bug. Selfishly at first: I thought about the ways that knitting would improve my broken wrist.

"I'll investigate lessons this afternoon," I vowed.

One evening and an exasperated yarn store owner later, I was diligently knitting a scarf again. I had pulled out the dusty, ivory scarf from years ago, but I soon found out that our new Collie puppy used the project as a chew toy. By now, our family finances had improved to the point where I could pay for a cashmere yarn that didn't pull apart or protest noisily.

Within a week, I bound off my scarf, and then I absently rubbed my throbbing wrist. While the scarf was a little lopsided and my tension control was lacking, I thought it was a thing of beauty.

"Is your wrist okay?" My husband inquired over strands of *The West Wing*'s opening song. Then he noticed the finished scarf, "It's beautiful. You going to wear it?"

I thought for a moment, "No, I'm going to give [it] to someone who needs it."

"Okay." He returned his attention back to the trials of President Bartlett, his mind already elsewhere.

No matter. As I eagerly dove into my yarn stash to start my next knitting project, I knew that Ava would approve.

CHARITY

EXCERPTS FROM AN INTERVIEW WITH
MISS EMMA WILLIS (CALLED AUNT EMMA)

CONCORD, NORTH CAROLINA
BY MURIEL L. WOLFF
SEPTEMBER 21, 1938

Aunt Emma Willis is very proud of being eighty-one years old. She is proud too that she doesn't have to wear glasses, even for reading, and that she still has her own teeth. If you ask her about cotton mills she will say quite casually in her high, thready voice, "I worked in a cotton mill for sixty-three years, but I never did care for it much. I had to quit six years ago when I had a bad case of the grippe."

Now that the weather is cool she sits in her walnut rocker by the window and knits lace from spool thread. "I just make up the patterns," she will explain, "and every time I knit a long piece I change because I get tired of doing the same one." For making enough lace to go on a pair of pillowcases (between eighty and ninety yards) she charges 50¢ and supplies the thread. This is the only money she can earn now.

But Aunt Emma is not doleful about it. With a sly smile on her face she will tell you quietly that she "lives on charity." Then her gray eyes twinkle as she says, "I'm just like everybody else now, letting the government support me. Before they gave me my old age pension, my church and the folks I knowd here kept me going..."

Everything about her person was precise—her dark voile dress with the checked apron tied tightly over it; her hair, carefully parted in the middle and looped back on either side so that the delicate gold crosses in her ears were visible. Her face was remarkable—long, straight featured, and intelligent. Behind her quiet reserve was the humor that occasionally showed in her eyes or the manner in which she made a remark.

It was not easy to get Aunt Emma to tell about herself. She was more interested in talking of the Mormons, her preacher, what had been happening in town or in reminiscing about Concord in the old days...

"When the war came and Pa went off to fight, I was so little I just can't remember much about it. But law, I'll never forget when the Yankees burned Salisbury. I wasn't but four years old but to this day I can remember how the sky looked that night—it was red all over one side. The Yankees never did hurt us; I guess they must have knowd my Grandfather. Pa came back from the war, but he died not so long after that. I had to go to work to support the family. There was my mother, who had the heart trouble; my little sister and little brother; and my old aunt who couldn't walk a step for twelve years before she died...

"When I was twelve, I started work in the old McDonald Mill that had been running here in town since before the war. It was the only cotton mill in Concord then. I went to work every morning at six and stayed until seven in the evening. They paid 35¢ a day. But law, in those days people didn't mind work—we had a good time. Many a night I would come in from the mill, wash my face, put on my hat and go off to choir practice or somewhere. I was young and strong so I didn't get tired..."

Once during our conversation Aunt Emma made a remark without her usual shy little smile. "There's something I've been studying about," and she put down her knitting. "I spent all my life working as hard as I could, but now I've got so I can't go anymore. You just look at the rich people this town has—people who've got plenty and more than they can ever use. It looks to me like the town ought to take care of the old people who can't help theirselves anymore..."

Credit: Library of Congress, Manuscript Division, WPA Federal Writers' Project Collection

Knitting class, Henry Street Settlement. Location: New York, New York, by Lewis Wickes Hine, 1910.
Credit: Library of Congress, Prints & Photographs Division, National Child Labor Committee Collection, reproduction #LC-DIG-nclc-04574

The settlement movement began in the late nineteenth century in order to address health problems among residents of growing slum populations in cities such as London, New York, and Chicago. At New York City's Henry Street Settlement, nurse and social reformer Lillian Wald took in immigrant children and gave them food, medicine, and education that were elsewhere unavailable to them. Much of the education, for children as well as neighborhood residents at large, was based on sanitary health, mental hygiene, and home economics. As is evidenced by this photo, knitting—both as a craft and a means to an economic boost—was part of some students' curriculum.

Sources: Thomas Lannon, Manuscripts Specialist, New York Public Library; Linnea M. Anderson, Assistant Archivist, Social Welfare History Archives, University of Minnesota

Knitting Through... Illness

SOFIA'S HANDS
BY ALEXANDRA HALPIN

Growing up in San Francisco, with my Italian relatives in close proximity, I learned the skills of surviving in domestic tranquility: sewing, knitting, crocheting, and cooking. Four generations of my mother's family settled in Russian Hill. Big Nana—my great-grandmother Sofia—lived with my great aunt and uncle around the corner; my grandparents lived in the flat above ours. They had no intention of returning to the small mountain village in Calabria where their ancestors had flourished. As a girl, I believed that my world was fully formed, and that adventure travel was exotic and unnecessary. Nevertheless, the stories of Jack London, Rudyard Kipling, and Jules Verne excited my nascent imagination.

In the spring of 1999, my husband Paul and I planned our annual vacation together. We had both been dreaming of visiting Alaska for years. Since childhood, I had ravenously read stories of the icy tundra, fiery wildflowers, and caribou; these things were as foreign to me as snow to any child born in coastal California. Paul had researched Alaska in his youth and intended to homestead there. He had acquired the best rugged outfitting he could afford, including a bear rifle that I could barely lift, and many clothes made of Gortex.

The previous summer, Paul and I had camped at Whiskeytown Lake a few miles outside of Redding, California. It was a five-hour drive from the Bay Area, and we hauled a truck-bed full of outdoor gear and a boat. With our tent, sleeping bags, cooking and fishing gear, we puttered to the other side of the lake in the boat and left our truck behind. The woods were full of bear, and the fish were plentiful. After this experience, we wondered if camping in the rugged Denali wilderness was really so far-fetched.

Alaska became our mantra. Every day, we talked about how, what, and when; soon, we had booked our travel. Everything was in place for our trip in late August. As summer approached, we dreamt of fireweed, grizzly bears, and glacial rivers.

That spring was also full of trepidation. We had been receiving calls late at night from Paul's mom, Rose Lee. Someone was in the house. Someone had stolen her money. She heard noises in the backyard. She heard voices. Something wasn't right. She had called 911 a couple of times, but no intruder was discovered prowling in the bushes. At first, we thought these were hallucinations brought on by her medication. She was a sprightly seventy-six years old and an unrelenting world traveler who had been living on her own since her husband died in 1981. We were somewhat relieved when her medication was adjusted and the hallucinations seemed to fade.

August finally arrived, and we flew to Alaska. While camping in Denali, we photographed bears splashing in the Teklanika River and watched ptarmigan sprint across the road like pheasants. Caribou lumbered across our path as we hiked from Polychrome Pass to Toklat River. We stepped in the shallow impressions of bear paw prints that were made recently enough to give us pause. This was the real frontier where nature governed.

During our travels, we discovered a parcel of land for sale on a secluded road. A modest wooden bridge crossed over the neighboring duck pond and led from the road to a rustic house. Abundant fireweed bloomed in tall stalks of red and purple the colors of the Alaskan twilight. At the edge of the pond, with our backs to civilization, we considered the pros and cons of living in Alaska's wild hinterland. Our family was in California. How often would we see them if we left everything behind and came to live here? We stepped away, looking over our shoulders at the bucolic setting, with mixed feelings.

On the way back to Anchorage, Paul and I visited the Matanuska Valley and the Musk Ox Farm in Palmer, home to the unique Oomingmak cooperative. [See Donna Druchunas's essay on pg 128.] This knitting cooperative produces delicate, warm-knitted items from qiviut, the fine under-wool of the musk ox, to supplement the income of their subsistence communities. Displayed there in the wilderness the lace of so many experienced hands drew me back to knitting. It was an art that I had learned as a child from my great-grandmother Sofia, my great-aunt Florence, and my grandmother Charlotte—extraordinary needlewomen who had imparted their knowledge to me with ease and gentility. I had never stopped knitting, but by the late 1990s, it was something I did only occasionally, to proffer a gift to an expectant mother or to make a warm sweater or scarf. I felt a kinship with the Oomingmak ladies who incorporated their traditional motifs into their designs. Each knitted smoke ring and scarf was carefully executed, and I recognized that the skill I had learned as a child was admired and valued here. I picked up the tiny sample skeins of qiviut and wondered how many I would need to make a sweater. Too many! Hundreds of dollars! No, the wool and alpaca at home in my knitting basket would have to suffice.

When Paul and I returned to California, we gleefully went about the tasks of making photo books of our vacation and decorating our lives with memorabilia. Our small San Bruno apartment was on a hill overlooking a valley of neat suburban homes with mountains in the distance—diminutive mounds in contrast with the mammoth, snow-capped peaks that had astounded us in Denali. We wistfully admired the photographs we had taken of the rustic cabin in the wilderness; its mere existence jeered our decision to return to city life.

Then one night, we got another call. Rose Lee whispered that someone was in the house. Paul advised her to call 911, and he looked at me with his own mounting alarm. Something was definitely wrong.

When the police arrived, they found that Rose Lee had crawled from her bedroom to the front door. They helped her into a chair, searched the house and garden, and found nothing amiss. She was breathless, and the paramedics took her to the hospital as a precaution. Paul knew it was time to find out what was happening. After a few tests, a neurologist gave the diagnosis of Alzheimer's disease. Paul's father had died of the same horrific affliction; both Paul and his mother knew what bleakness lay in the imminent future.

As for me, I was not ready for the commitment of caring for an elderly person who needed an increasing amount of assistance. I was thirty-seven years old. My own mother had liver disease brought on by hepatitis C, contracted through a blood transfusion in the early 1980s, and was seeing doctors and specialists. My father was by her side, but I felt a looming sense of urgency as her health declined. By October, I knew the memory of the freedom I had savored in Alaska that summer would have to last a long time.

Paul and I talked about our options. He was already taking more time off from work than he ever thought he would in order to care for his mother. I was worried about our mothers and our future. By November, we made the decision to move in with Rose Lee. She had lost the ability to take her medications on her own, and her night frights had returned.

We welcomed the New Year on the balcony of our apartment with champagne. Fireworks sparkled among the homes in the valley beyond our plastic cups. By then, the apartment was empty of furnishings. We had moved everything, one truckload at a time, to my mother-in-law's house, filling her garage with our belongings. Her guestroom had been converted to our bedroom with new paint as well as our pictures and lamps. The next day, the first day of the new millennium, our lives would change significantly.

In the beginning, we had no routine. The house was new to me but not to Paul, who had been raised in it. He knew every cranny, every book and spoon. I felt like a visitor who had come to stay awhile. My books were crammed onto a few bookshelves in our small bedroom; my spoons were in a box in the garage. My yarn was carefully packed away in a large plastic tub, along with all the tools and books of my craft. The heirloom handmade bedspreads and tablecloths I had inherited from my great-grandmother Sofia were stored prudently in my cedar chest.

Within a couple of months, my own mother's condition worsened, though I still had no idea how deeply this would affect me. She had been placed on the liver transplant list, and she kept most of the frightening details to herself. It was not until she was hospitalized in May that I realized her life was precariously close to ending.

Engrossed in family matters, I was acutely aware of my lack of creative stimuli. Paul quit his job to stay at home full-time with his mother, and my misguided conscience forbade me from enjoying outside activities without him. I ravaged the Internet looking for caregiving support groups and found that accessing them deepened the awareness of my current situation. What I needed was a creative outlet to distract me from the persistent ache of worry.

I reclaimed my yarn and craft books from their temporary home in the garage and began researching stitch patterns for an afghan. It would be the first I had made in years. I spent hours searching for just the right wool and found it on the Internet at Beaverslide Dry Goods, a small Montana sheep ranch. The box of heathery wool arrived with all the colors of earth and sky: browns, greens, blues, and berries. I caressed each skein before winding it into a ball the old-fashioned way, with a skein draped around the back of a chair. I began wrapping the yarn in a figure eight around my thumb and forefinger, then wrapped it loosely into a ball, meditating to the rhythm of my hands moving in familiar circles.

I remembered sitting next to my great-grandmother Sofia as she rocked in her chair, and the gentle cadence of her hands as she made an intricate lacy bureau scarf. Sofia spoke Italian and very little English. She instructed me with her hands and nodded her head when I mimicked her fluid movements. Now, as I knitted the afghan, I wondered if my work would someday be cherished in the way I treasured things made by Sofia. In the corner of the afghan, I stitched "PS" (S for Sandy, my family's nickname for me), an affirmation of the love Paul and I shared for each other that would strengthen us in the troubling months ahead. No longer did I need a special occasion to knit. I knit because it was freeing and it compensated for the restrictions that were now imposed on my life.

By this time, I had learned my way around my new habitat and figured out how to combine my life with my mother-in-law's in every detail. Drawers were reorganized, closets shuffled. My spoons were now in the kitchen drawer with hers.

Despite my initial feelings of disorientation in Rose Lee's house, I always felt welcome in it. Rose Lee was a Southern woman, and her hospitality was indisputable. She took pride in her appearance and her immaculate surroundings. She had a standing appointment with her local hairdresser, and her short, silvery hair was styled into a tidy coif every Saturday. It was disturbing to see her well-ordered life begin to deteriorate. She forgot where things were and where to put things away. She forgot how to unlatch the back door to the garden. She forgot that she had only one dog, not two.

After a few months, Paul and I inexplicably came down with an itchy rash. One morning, we discovered the cause: A poof of soap billowed out of the dryer vent, into the backyard, coating the landscaping with white powder. Rose Lee had been adding soap to the dryer, and our clothes were coated with invisible soap dust. We decided it was time for us to control laundry privileges. Rose Lee perceived this as yet another defeat but, as her southern manners dictated, she accepted the change and we continued to live in harmony.

Knitting annexed my attention in the evenings. I glanced up occasionally to see Rose Lee pacing across the living room, back and forth, or peeking out the windows and doors, as if she were waiting for the familiar intruder to find his way back inside. We tried to ignore the hallucinations or change the subject when they occurred. Sometimes the pillows were people, sitting wordlessly, waiting for their tea. Sometimes a sweater hanging on a bedpost was a little girl who had no place else to go. Sometimes a shadow was a man lounging in a corner near the fireplace, callously snubbing us.

Other times, a familiar tune aroused memories of happier occasions, and Rose Lee trotted across the floor beaming with joy. We danced like carefree children who were unfettered by convention. Sometimes, we sat and laughed at old movies together. Although she could no longer express herself verbally, her laughter made us believe that we were doing something right. When I was engrossed in my knitting, sometimes she would reach out to touch it like a child. I could see the appreciation in her pale green-grey eyes, which were just like Paul's. In her youth and until her diagnosis, Rose Lee was an avid traveler who had not been interested in learning the home arts of knitting or sewing. Even so, she admired the skill and patience of stitching, and her smile conveyed her affection. I wondered what I would do in my old age if I could not make my hands remember what to do. What would I do if I could not knit anymore? I could see the stitches in my head. Maybe I would think about them, creating imaginary garments never to touch them.

In the meantime, I had been visiting my mother in the hospital daily. We knew that if a transplant donor was not found quickly, she would not make it through the summer. Miraculously, she did receive a transplant, but shortly afterward she succumbed to an infection. In August of 2000, I lost my greatest confidante and champion. She had been through several surgeries and spent months in the hospital. My father was healthy but emotionally exhausted, and in the months and years that followed, I helped him discover his new direction in life.

Gradually, Rose Lee became less able to care for herself and required more and more assistance with the simple tasks of daily living. Paul bore the majority of that dire responsibility. We had chosen our path, and Paul and I were determined to see it through to the end.

In 2002, I came upon Knitter's Review, a web forum for knitters, and began reading the postings daily. Through the forum, I connected with local knitters and co-founded a knitting group called the Bay Area Wool Divas (BAWDies). We first met in the Financial District in San Francisco, and later we had a home at Valencia Street Books. The knitters I met soon became my friends. We shared not only our mutual love for knitting, but stories of our lives and tribulations of day-to-day living. Most often, the talk was about our latest projects, new knitting books, and designers. For a little while each week, the BAWDies gave me respite from caregiving.

When Rose Lee passed away in 2003, some of my new knitting friends were the first to comfort me. They, as well as family and friends, shared their concern and advice as Paul and I went through one of the most difficult periods in our lives. With this objective network of support, I was able to look gratefully in a new, promising direction. I grieved for the losses we experienced and thanked God for the blessings of our lives—our family and friends.

Life did not begin anew all at once. But slowly, parts of my persona that I had put aside began to reemerge. I learned to take pleasure in simple freedoms, including all the joys of knitting.

The BAWDies were growing in number, so I organized events and field trips for them, including a visit to Alpacas by the Sea, an alpaca farm in Montara, California, and an afternoon knitting cruise on the Golden Gate Ferry in San Francisco Bay. I began to test knitting for designers and contracted to knit a sweater for Teva Durham's book, *Loop-d-Loop*.

I was knitting all the time now. Sometimes when I was on my way to work, I would have unexpected conversations with people on the train about my knitting. As I was standing and knitting in the station one day, a driver came up to me and said, "My wife has been knitting up a storm lately. She knits blankets for preemie babies."

"I knit hats for cancer patients," I mentioned, pausing to see if I had dropped a stitch. He just smiled at the project in my hands. It wasn't a hat, but he didn't need to know that. I had been contributing hats to another group, the Stitching Sisters in El Granada, who donated the hats to a local cancer center.

Another day, I sat in my usual seat, in the first car next to the rear exit door, and pulled out a sweater in progress. A young woman embarked after me with a loop of burgundy yarn sagging between her hands and her black shoulder bag. Her needles were silent bamboo and mine were slippery silver. She sat across from me, knitting and not speaking, but we comfortably communicated our contentment.

As city dwellers, everyone in my family from Big Nana Sofia to me rode the cable cars, buses, and trolleys in San Francisco at one time or another. To the best of my recollection, my knitting and crocheting relatives never took their needlework on the buses or outside their homes, unless it was to attend a knitting or sewing bee. When Sofia would come to visit us on an ordinary day, she would sit on the sofa twiddling her thumbs. "Big" Nana was barely five feet tall with snow white hair and tiny gold-rimmed eyeglasses. Her hands were soft and smooth with tapering, wrinkled fingers that had been tempered by the hard work of raising her seven children, washing, cooking, and cleaning. She would smile and twiddle, with nothing to keep her hands occupied. Now when I am without my knitting on a bus or anywhere else, I find myself twiddling, remembering her lovely unencumbered hands.

Knitting at home, our dog Duke sits by my feet, his long, silky white hair splayed across my toes. When he senses I am ready for a break, he stands and yawns. I put the work down and stand and stretch too.

On a particularly grey day, I opened my cedar chest and found the boxes of ancient doilies, tablecloths, and bedspreads made by Sofia. Perfect, neatly finished, with delicate arrangements of stitches, these masterworks were her expressions, communicated to me in the present. Underneath the boxes was an afghan she had made for me as a child, in lemon yellow and lime green, colors I had loved. As I held it in my hands, I recalled those girlhood years on Russian Hill and Big Nana's angelic smile. Paul's mother and my mother were gone now, but their legacy of love and family was ours to cherish and nurture. I pulled the afghan out and sat with it around me, remembering childhood hugs and kisses, and hands that showed me how to make beautiful things.

Woman knitting, Washington, D.C., by John Vachon, 1941. *Credit: Library of Congress, Prints & Photographs Division, FSA/OWI Collection, reproduction #LC-USF34-014621-D DLC*

Knitting Through It

Excerpt from "Knitting Sale-Socks,"
The Atlantic Monthly, Volume 7,
Issue 40, February 1861

We've got a cow and the filly and some sheep; and mother shears and cards, and Lurindy spins, I can't spin, it makes my head swim, and I knit, knit socks and sell them. Sometimes I have needles almost as big as a pipe-stem, and choose the coarse, uneven yarn of the thruins, and the work goes off like machinery. Why, I can knit two pair, and sometimes three, a day, and get just as much for them as I do for the nice ones, they're warm. But when I want to knit well, as I did the day Aunt Mimy was in, I take my best blue needles and my fine white yarn from the long wool, and it takes me from daybreak till sundown to knit one pair. I don't know why Aunt Jemimy should have said what she did about my socks; I'm sure Stephen hadn't been any nearer them than he had to the cabbage-bag Lurindy was netting, and there wasn't such a nice knitter in town as I . . .

I made the needles fly while mother was gone for the doctor. By-and-by I heard a knock up in Stephen's room, I suppose he wanted something, but Lurindy didn't hear it, and I didn't so much want to go, so I sat still and began to count out loud the stitches to my narrowings. By-and-by he knocked again. Lurindy, says I, ant that Steve a-knocking? Yes, says she, why don't you go? for I had been tending him a good deal that day. Well, says I, there's a number of reasons; one is, I'm just binding off my heel.

Lurindy looked at me a minute... Well, Emmy, says she, if you like a smooth skin more than a smooth conscience, you're welcome, and went upstairs herself.

Credit: Library of Congress, The Nineteenth Century in Print: The Making of America in Books and Periodicals

Hélène Magnússon wearing her Hammer Rose
Pattern Vest.

Credit: Hélène Magnússon

Knitting Through It

Three Stitches per Second
By Hélène Magnússon

When I was about seven years old, my mother taught me how to knit. My knitting was full of inexplicable holes, and as the rows progressed, the stitches decreased in number and were so tight that I could no longer move the needles. It was so frustrating.

My father didn't knit, but he smoked. As a child, I devoted myself to all sorts of experiments to dissuade him from it. For example, I would have him close his eyes and then I would present him with a cigarette; sometimes it was unlit, sometimes it was lit. This was supposed to demonstrate to him that he couldn't tell the difference—he couldn't—and to this he would answer: "And so what?" I also lectured him each time he lit a cigarette in front of me, which was often.

As for the knitting, I was determined to get it—I have always liked all sorts of handwork. So one day I cast on ten stitches and counted and recounted at every row, row after row, until I finally made progress. After four meters, I knew how to knit. I knit for my dolls: bags and blankets, a green dress, a red-and-white flamenco dress.

Meanwhile, I continued my anti-tobacco experiments until one day, exasperated, my father handed me his cigarette and said, "Here, try this. You'll see." I liked it right away. From then on, I spent privileged moments with my father smoking our evening cigarette in the garden and hiding from my mother. I must have been fourteen years old.

In high school, all the popular kids smoked. This was tough. As an adolescent, I affirmed my independence not by opposing my parents but by opposing my peers. So, I systematically refused all offers of cigarettes, turning up my nose and standing up straight when they chuckled and leered. I would like to be able to write that this ruse worked for many years, but unfortunately that was not the case with tobacco. Very quickly, one cigarette a day was not enough to satisfy me, and I began to smoke in secret.

Craving nicotine, it became harder and harder for me to refuse the smokes that were constantly offered at school. I hid the secret from my father, so that he could have a clear conscience about it. I also hid my smoking from the prefects and from my classmates, which made the task of keeping it secret rather difficult, although exciting. After a few months, I cracked and accepted my first official cigarette. Admitted into the clan of smokers, I fell back into my knitting as if trying *not* to fit in with them; knitting made me different. I systematically presented myself at parties with my knitting, again by means of opposition, amused by the comments I would get about looking like a grandmother, which I disdainfully disregarded.

I didn't know how to knit and smoke. I smoked less than I knit, and I only knit in public.

At university, I started out studying law, more as something to do with myself than as a true vocation. I was utterly bored. To make time pass quicker, I knit little figures and animals that were ten centimeters high to give to friends. One friend was going to London, so I knit him a beefeater. Another friend—a Leo—was turning thirty, so I knit him a little lion. Those gifts were much appreciated. The thirty-year-old friend was especially moved because he thought mine was the only gift he received that really came from the heart. He told me he would give it to his son— when and if he had one.

I knit during lectures, and I smoked during breaks. I wasn't so much a great knitter as a great smoker. I could take or leave knitting, but I smoked like a chimney.

My studies were coming to an end, and I decided to quit smoking if I passed the French equivalent of the LSAT (CAPA—Capacité d'Aptitude á la Profession Avocat) on the first try. Completely unaware of the depth of my dependency, I bragged out loud that quitting was just a matter of willpower. The day of the results, I was therefore in tears as I received my diploma. Deprived as much of nicotine as of will, I spent many hours feeling sorry for myself and describing to anyone who wanted to listen—or didn't—all the symptoms of my discomfort and the details of my ill-being. My friends were amused at first, then weary, finally exasperated. By evening, I went back on my promise. I lit my first cigarette, breathed at last, and promised never to quit smoking again.

Now a lawyer, I was as bored as ever. I smoked for longer periods at a time. I no longer had time to knit because I was working so hard, often late into the night and on weekends.

In 1995, I took a trip to Iceland. After I returned home to France, I took an extra week of vacation, during which I knit non-stop (except for cigarette breaks) because I finally had the time and needed to think in peace. At the end of the week, I gave my resignation at work and flew back to Iceland; I had fallen in love with the country. Later, after I'd moved there, I met my future husband. Reneging on my promise of several years earlier, I decided once again to quit smoking. It was my boyfriend's idea; he convinced me we could stop smoking together. This time, I was resolved and I wasn't alone. I tried to do it the right way by choosing a period of calm and finding my way to a Chinese acupuncturist. A little bead of metal taped to my ear was supposed to cause me unbearable headaches with every inhalation of tobacco. I symbolically threw my pack of cigarettes into the trash.

I didn't keep a cool head for long. I was quickly assailed by existential questions: "If I don't smoke, what am I going to do with my life?" "Does life have any meaning if I can't have a smoke?" That first night, my boyfriend slept on the sofa—I had gone completely crazy without my cigarettes, and we'd had a fight. Around 4:00 AM, I shut the door of our apartment and broke into a crazy run through the streets in my nightgown, heading for my boyfriend's grandfather's cellar. It had a special room in it where the grandfather would drink his beer and smoke. I knew where the key to the basement was, and where inside to find what I was looking for. I rummaged in the big, black ashtray to collect a few left-over butts, from which I extracted the tobacco in order to roll something like a cigarette. Disgusting. The butts were menthol, which I hated. But they were exactly what I needed to survive the rest of the night, until the nearest shop opened.

I cursed this country, where everything was closed at night. I cursed the acupuncturist who convinced me to throw away an almost-full pack of cigarettes. I cursed my boyfriend, who had quit smoking too and couldn't back me up with one little cigarette. At the end of the next day, I tore away the acupuncture bead that was pressed against my ear that gave me such headaches with every puff—I forgot that this was supposed to be the whole idea. The following night, I used all my charms to convince my boyfriend to start smoking again, too.

"It has to be a shared act, something we do together," I told him. Actually, I kind of threatened him: If he wouldn't go back on his decision to quit smoking, I would break up with him!

We didn't break up; we got married. By this point, I hadn't been knitting for a while. It was so exciting to start a new life in Iceland, and there was so much to do and to learn. I had no time to be bored and no need to calm down. We moved abroad, to Oxford, for a year. My husband was pursuing an advanced degree in Jurisprudence— the philosophy of law. I knew that as a non-student, I would become rather lonely on campus, so I decided to take along a big knitting project to fill my evenings. It had to be big enough to last the whole year in Oxford. I chose a reproduction of an Icelandic woven blanket from the seventeenth century, which I thought was beautiful. The chart had originally been made for cross stitch. During this period, I used my loneliness to reflect on my life and to try to figure out what I was going to do with it, since I had completely given up law. I would knit the blanket and smoke and think every evening while my husband would read and smoke and study.

It was in the middle of knitting a row of the blanket that the possibility occurred to me that this knitting, which occupied my hands, could be something more than a hobby. At this time, the worlds of textiles and design were completely unknown to me—I had been ignorant of their very existence. Very quickly, I decided to make inquiries into what possibilities there were for school in Iceland, discovered that I could study textile design, made a round-trip to Reykjavík, and wound up taking the entrance exam for what is now known as the Iceland Academy of the Arts.

On February 26, 1998, I got sick with a bad flu that kept me in bed for a number of days. For the first time in my life, I just couldn't smoke. I had always smoked when I was sick in the past—had to get my nicotine no matter what. But this time, it was like five talons on an invisible hand were cutting my throat. Not even a clean cut, but one that would be made by a dull, rusty knife. At the first sign of withdrawal, I made my husband buy me a pack of nicotine gum, and so I was able to survive for some days without cigarettes.

I did not decide to quit smoking; I just allowed myself to see if I could bear one more day without a cigarette. Two days became three, then four. I finally made it out of bed. On my feet, I was still a nicotine addict. I loved taking out the pack, lighting a cigarette, bringing it to my mouth, delicately squeezing it with two fingers, letting my hand hang carelessly, my eyes barely closed, my lips half-open, my head leaning imperceptibly back, my hot breath lost in wisps of blue smoke, the little dry tap on the edge of the ashtray. Without smoking, the rhythm of my days was upset; I missed my routine, my little habits terribly. Bad breath, headaches, shortness of breath, my pasty tongue in the morning, my yellowing fingers, the odor of stale cat pee coming from the ashtray, my smoke-saturated clothes, my irritated eyes, the irritating consciousness of my dependency, my dull skin, the taste of burned paper in my mouth—I missed all that too.

The withdrawal didn't go smoothly and often approached crisis. As soon as a crisis began, I put a piece of nicotine gum in my mouth, rushed headlong for my knitting, and knitted frenetically—five stitches, one row, one minute, two rows, my heart beating fast and my hands damp, until it passed. Then a second crisis would begin, too soon to take another piece of nicotine gum. I threw myself into my knitting and knit like I'd entered a trance. One stitch, one second, two stitches, two seconds. At full speed, I chewed the gum that had been completely emptied of its nicotine. Ten rows a minute. I counted the stitches aloud: Twelve stitches, three stitches a second. I couldn't keep this pace up for very long. I don't believe that I would be capable of knitting so quickly today. Then the crisis was over. There I was like a madwoman, chewing like crazy and panting out numbers—fifty-six stitches—my body tensed, bent forward, with my hands shaking, one stitch dropped—123 stitches—my mouth bloody because I'd bitten my tongue—354 stitches.

Knitting was not always enough to help me get through a crisis. When the nicotine in the gum was all used up, I would start salivating abundantly. Then I would indulge in a piece of chocolate. Knitting may be good for your joints and good for your peace of mind, but it doesn't give you much exercise. I started to put on kilos.

458 stitches—the blanket advanced quickly.

My husband smoked in his office at home, completely bundled up, because I insisted that from now on we had to keep a window open.

I knit in the day through all my breaks at work at Oxford's Alliance Française, where I was teaching French—not my cup of tea. I knit the whole evening until late, and I sometimes got up in the night, "Just to knit a little." When my husband and I went out, I always showed up with my needles to help me resist an eventual, inevitable temptation. I would keep them in my bag until there was an emergency. I had some difficult moments, like drinking my first glass of wine without a cigarette. The menthol and fruity flavors of nicotine gum don't really go with wine, or for that matter, coffee. In fact, I didn't like nicotine gum at all. I would force it into my mouth only to chew the nicotine out of it; after all, it is just a substitute for smoking, which keeps the longing for cigarettes alive.

After three months, I slowly reduced my consumption of the gum and that summer, I finished knitting the blanket. It was magnificent and as much of an accomplishment as quitting smoking. Both filled me with pride. I had put on ten kilos and officially become an ex-smoker. I kept a piece of nicotine gum in my pocket for one year, just in case. My knitting never left me.

At the end of the summer, I started my new studies in textile design. I wasn't bored at all. I didn't knit much—just for one knitting class that was part of the school curriculum. I never asked for a light anymore and no one asked me for one, either. I began to miss the complicity of smokers squeezed together on a tiny balcony or in a doorway, even when outside it was raining or cold or both—I had gotten to know so many people through smoking. I also stopped going to bars because I couldn't stand the smoke anymore; it irritated my throat horribly and left me hoarse in the morning. The first paper I had to write for school was a challenge because I had always smoked before, and I considered smoking to be part of the writing process. I was convinced my brain couldn't work without the nicotine. But I drew up my knitting needles, and for this challenge, too, everything was alright.

Now I have written a whole book about knitting. I have absolutely no longing for cigarettes and don't miss anything about it. My husband is still struggling, though. He stopped smoking the same year I did, the summer after his exams. He chewed nicotine gum for two years, started smoking cigars, tried medication, started nicotine gum again, then medication again, then cigars, then gum. He finally quit in the summer of 2006. But, a week before writing this, I smelled cigar smoke in his hair, and I caught him smoking a cigar outside two days later.

Sylvía, my oldest daughter, who is six years old, asked me to teach her how to knit. She is doing very well at it. She's making a scarf for her teddy bear and has already knit some thirty-five centimeters. There is just one hole in it and one extra stitch. I am very proud of her. If she is asked to do some other task while she's in the middle of knitting, she says, "I'm coming—I'm finishing a row!" just like me, and

I find it so cute. Theodóra, my second daughter, four years old, says she is too small to learn knitting but she wants me to teach her when she is five. I will. Henrietta, my third daughter who is sixteen months old, is showing a lot of interest in both the needles and the yarn. Sylvía and I must hide our knitting to keep her from playing with it—and unraveling it.

I hope none of them will smoke!

Translated from the French by Lela Nargi & Robert Cowan

A pair of soft Icelandic shoes with knitted insoles—these worn for special occasions.

Reproduced by permission from Hélène Magnússon, Rósaleppaprjón í n´yju ljósi (Icelandic Color Knitting: Rose Pattern Insert Knitting in a New Light) (Reykjavík, IS: Salka, 2006), cover.

HAMMER ROSE VEST

This is inspired by old woolen shoe inserts displaying a hammer rose motif, belonging to the National Museum of Iceland's Ethnological Collections.

Size: S (M) L
Width: Approx. 102 (112) 120 centimeters, 40.2 (44) 47.2 inches
Length: Approx. 54 (55) 58 centimeters, 21.3 (21.7) 22.8 inches
Materials: Loðband - einband from Ístex (www.istex.is) 100 % new Icelandic wool, 50 gr ball equal approx 150 meters (164 yards/492 feet). It can be ordered from the Handknitting Association of Iceland (www.handknit.is/en/user/cat/show/11/37)

- white 0851, 3 (3) 4 balls
- black 0059, 2 balls
- violet 9933, 1 ball
- bright red 0078, 1 ball, special-dye, available at the Handknitting Association of Iceland
- green 9823, 1 ball, special-dye, available at the Handknitting Association of Iceland
(www.handknit.is/en/user/cat/show/11/37)
- yellow 0995, 1 ball, special-dye, available at the Handknitting Association of Iceland
Needles: 4 (4½) 4½ millimeters, 6 (7) 7 U.S. needles, 3 millimeters (size C) crochet hook
Tension: 10x10 centimeters, 4" x 4" using garter stitch and

intarsia technique on 4 (4 ½) millimeters size 6 (size 7) needles equal 19 (18) sts and 21 (19) garters.
= 1 st and 1 garter
Knitting method: The vest is knitted back and forth using garter stitch and intarsia technique.
Garter stitch: 1 garter = 2 rows k worked back and forth
Picot edging: 1st row: crochet 1 slip st in the edge, *1 sc, repeat from*. 2nd row: crochet 1 slip st and then *1 picot (3 chain sts, 1 slip st in second chain st, 1 slip st in first chain st), pass over 2 sts, 1 sc in next st, repeat from*.

Front: Cast on 96 (96) 102 sts using 4 (4½) 4½ millimeter needles and white yarn. Knit pattern in garter st, beginning at the appropriate mark according to size. Repeat pattern from * to * to end of row and also from *–* upward. N.B.: = 1 st and 1 garter. When the front measures approx. 31 (32) 33 centimeters, 12.2 (12.6) 13 inches, shape armholes by casting off 6 sts on each side and continue decreasing 1 st in each garter five times and 1 st in every fifth garter three times. When the front measures approx. 47 (48) 51 centimeters, 18.5 (18.9) 20 inches, cast off for the neck opening 14 sts in the middle, then on each side 2 sts in each garter (three) four times. Knit each shoulder individually. When the front measures approx. 53 (54) 57 centimeters, 20.9 (21.3) 22.4 inches, shape shoulder by casting off 6 (6) 7 sts in each garter twice, then remaining sts.

Back: Knit the back like the front but don't start casting off for the neck opening until the back measures approx. 50 (51) 54 centimeters, 19.7 (20.1) 21.3 inches, then cast off

24 sts in the middle and on each side 1 st in each garter four times. Knit each shoulder individually. When the back measures approx. 53 (54) 57 centimeters, 20.9 (21.3) 22.4 inches, shape shoulder as on front.

Finishing: Sew shoulder seams. Sew side seams until there are 4 (4) 5 centimeters 1.6 (1.6) 2 inches left from the lower edge (slit). Crochet a picot edging using 3 millimeter hook (size C) and white yarn at the lower edge, around the armholes and around the neck opening. Darn in loose ends.

Reproduced by permission from Hélène Magnússon, *Rósaleppaprjón í n´yju Ijósi (Icelandic Color Knitting: Rose Pattern Insert Knitting in a New Light)* (Rey´kjavík, IS: Salka, 2006), page 102.

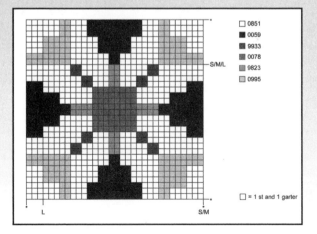

Knitting Through...
Grief

KNITTING LIFE, KNITTING LOVE
BY MARGARET BLANK

The house is quiet, so quiet. I turn on the television for background noise and something to sit in front of as I pick up my knitting. I've opened the cards, returned the phone calls, paid the bills, written a few more e-mails, and a couple of thank-you notes. Time now to unwind a wee bit. My knitting is more than relaxing, though; while it orders the motions of my fingers, it orchestrates my thoughts and subdues my anxieties, taking the sharp edges off grief.

I belong to the third generation of knitters in my family. Before me sailed two grandmothers and a step-Gran (though she preferred crochet), my mother, Mom's first cousin, and my father's sister.

Mom taught me to knit when I was eight or nine years old. Oddly, I don't remember ever seeing her knit, but she *must* have. There was evidence of it all 'round the house—sweaters for me and my step-siblings, mittens, hats, gloves, and scarves. She favored cables, which she used in hats, mitts, and gloves, and in the royal blue turtleneck that I wore into my early teens, despite the fact that it was singed from Girl Guide campfires and it had shrunk—or I had grown!

The first thing I learned was corking, also known as spool-knitting. Mom gave me colorful worsted-weight yarn to wind around the heads of nails that were hammered into a pudgy blue spool, about two inches around and three inches high. She taught me to hook the yarn over this foundation in such a way that a long, knitted tube was created. When it was long enough, I learned to take it off the corker and wind it into a spiral, securing it with small stitches in matching thread. *Et voila*: a potholder or a hot pad. I was relieved when she began to teach me "real" knitting because in the end, corking was boring. There didn't seem to be much future in potholders and hot pads.

I suspect I started with the usual garter-stitch square, but its appearance and size have departed my memory. My first *real* knitting project was a pair of mittens knit on two needles and sewn up one side. Each featured a cable up the back. There was no pattern for the cable; it came straight out of Mom's head.

It was about that time that I realized how creative my mother could be. As a young woman, she was wasp-waisted—seventeen inches around *without* a corset—and tall, so to get the svelte look she wanted from the knitted dresses that were so fashionable at the time, she would take the top and/or sleeves of one pattern and combine it with the skirt of another. There might be batwing sleeves substituted for arm-hugging set-in ones, or a gored skirt replacing a straight one, all in the name of fashion.

I soon realized that I had a reputation for quality, speed, and creativity to uphold, a solid tradition of knitting through life, regardless of what lay ahead.

My grandmothers knit first through necessity, clothing their families. This was especially true of my paternal grandmother. She was a farm wife with fewer resources and less access to store-bought items than my mother's mother, who lived in Montreal. She would have knit scarves, toques, and mittens for warmth during bitter Canadian winters, as well as socks and long stockings to keep boys' feet dry and girls' knees protected to and from school or the barns.

My mother's mother was widowed in her late forties, during the early years of the Great Depression. With no other source of income, she began to take in boarders. Rather than buy new, she made over clothes as required and knit the afghans, sweaters, socks, gloves, hats, and scarves her family needed. Mom once told me about the hand-knit stockings that Grandma D. made her—and how they collected burrs in the spring or snow bobbles in winter as Mom walked across the vacant lots between home and school.

My grandmothers, along with my mother, her cousin, and my aunt, knit through the war next. All made socks much in demand for the men "over there." The British-based Patons & Baldwin Company was the favorite supplier of patterns for what it called "service woollies" from its book, *Service Woollies for Air, Land and Sea*, co-published with Beehive in both the UK and Canada.[1] My father loved his hand-knit socks so much that he persuaded Mom to continue to make them for him upon his return home in 1946. After his death in 1952, she never knit another sock—except to show me how to do it. I treasure the pattern booklets she left me from this time—*Hand Knit Socks by Beehive, The Monarch Hand Knit Sock Book,* and *Hand Knit Socks by Regent,* all ranging in price from twenty to thirty-five cents!

In the early 1950s, my mother knit through grief. My father died when she was only seven weeks pregnant with me. She wanted to provide for her new baby, and to be soothed and distracted by a project. She chose a shawl featured on the cover of a Paton's book, *Heirloom, with Rose Medallions and Rose Petal Border,* advertised as 100 years old. I still have the shawl—used by my children and awaiting grandchildren—and the book of patterns. Meanwhile, my grandmothers eased their own grief by knitting hats and booties. Stored with the shawl is a fluffy "kitten" bonnet—pink, with ears and white angora trim—and another pink bonnet with a knitted face-framing ruffle. There was hope and love knit into every stitch.

Later in life, Mom knit through losing weight and quitting smoking—two challenges she decided to accomplish concurrently in order to bring down her soaring blood pressure. In the space of 52 weeks, she quit smoking, lost 40 pounds, and went off her blood pressure medication. She also quadrupled her knitting output in the process!

Once I married, Mom again knit through pregnancies—mine. I've tucked away a glorious yellow baby blanket with lace edging, a little green dress, and a tiny green sweater decorated with intarsia doggies, which all serve as memories of those years preserved for my children.

As my son and daughter grew, I knit for them as well. Mom went back to knitting for my stepsister and me because, as she put it, we were *her* kids and she decided that we had every right to enjoy hand-knits, too. I remember four sweaters from that time—an off-white pullover with wide neck and dolman sleeves that was trimmed with a then-revolutionary eyelash yarn, as if it were striped with fringe; a black cotton tunic accented with green and turquoise paisley shapes; and a denim cotton pullover that I wore out with love. The fourth I still have—a cabled pullover in deep cherry merino, with a roll collar and sleeves that are just a tad too short. Having no matching yarn with which to lengthen them, this sweater languishes on a shelf in my closet. But I can't bear to part with it altogether. I believe that the love knit into a garment can't be released unless the garment is worn. Perhaps someday I'll find a way to make over my pullover so that I can enfold myself in my Mom's love once more.

At the same time, my mother continued knitting for church bazaars and charity donations. She made little pullovers, cardigans, and mittens that sustained her through my stepfather's last illness; with him, she'd shared almost thirty-seven years of marriage.

Then she lost her sight. Alas, her fingers, stiff and insensitive due to arthritis, could not help her to knit through macular degeneration. She gave me the beginnings of a fifth sweater—a casual boat-neck pullover in colorful stripes of burgundy, rust, blue, and burnt orange in Jo Sharp merino. Eventually, I ripped out her dropped stitches and uneven stripes with every intention of beginning the sweater again. Somehow, I find myself unable to go back to it. Nearly five years after her death, it remains an Unfinished Object.

While Mom's eyesight was failing, so were my husband's kidneys—the result of living for more than thirty-five years with Type 1 diabetes. There were no organs available for transplant, and his health deteriorated steadily once he was on dialysis. He endured open heart surgery and angioplasty; laser eye surgery; one below-the-knee amputation, and another; and then loss of fine-motor finger movement, hearing, and short-term memory.

I took up my own knitting more fervently, as if to match the pace of his decline with the pace of my creations. I shared with Susan Gordon Lydon the sense that "... any fresh grief builds a pipeline to all the grief that's gone before."[2] I couldn't stop the work of my hands, as if it made some sense out of all of these losses, bringing order out of chaos. I knit sweaters for each of my children, which now included a son-in-law and his sisters. I knit prayer shawls and chemo caps, preemie caps and crib blankets, toddlers' sweaters, and afghan squares.

Its rhythm and obvious productivity means that knitting remained my favorite form of creativity. I knit through each and every day, beginning with my early morning walks, which fascinated and amused my neighbors and fellow-knitters alike. I knit through trips to the hospital, in doctors' waiting rooms, through chats with my husband's diabetologist, nephrologist, and/or physical therapist. I knit through his massages and home care nurses' visits. I knit through evenings as he dozed in front of the television. I knit on the handi-bus while accompanying him to the zoo, a hockey game, or a festival in a downtown park.

I dubbed 2006, "The Year of the Sock." Beginning in January, I knit a pair every two weeks, including two pairs of stump socks for my husband in a stretchy cotton blend that he loved and wore constantly. At a time when "The Disease" had taken over so much of our lives, making the stump socks was a diversion (I had to design my own pattern, a first for me). It was also a new and particularly special way I could show him my love.

I knit through retreats when I took respite from care giving. I knit through the laughter we shared together, and I knit through the tears I cry alone.

Howard died over a month ago, and the children are grown and gone. Time stretches before me like a Saskatchewan wheat field... and still I knit, wondering and waiting for life to begin again.

[1] Scott, Shirley A., "What Canadians Knit," *Canada Knits: Craft and Comfort in a Northern Land*. Toronto: McGraw-Hill Ryerson, 1990.

[2] Lydon, Susan Gordon. *Knitting Heaven and Earth*. New York: Broadway Books, 2005.

Knitting Through... Work

This little girl like many others in this state is so small she has to stand on a box to reach her machine. She is regularly employed as a knitter in London [i.e., Loudon?] Hosiery Mills. Said she did not know how long she had worked there. Location: Loudon, Tennessee, by Lewis Wickes Hine, 1910 December.

Notes: Attribution to Hine based on provenance.

There is both a Loudon and a London, Tennessee. UMBC records similar photos as "Loudon," however.

Credit: Library of Congress, Prints & Photographs Division, National Child Labor Committee Collection, reproduction #LC-DIG-nclc-02003

EXCERPTS FROM AN INTERVIEW
WITH ALICE CANDLE

CONCORD, NORTH CAROLINA
BY MURIEL L WOLFF
SEPTEMBER 2, 1938

"Law, I reckon I was born to work in a mill. I started when I was ten year old and I aim to keep right on jest as long as I'm able. I'd a-heap rather do it then housework."

Alice Candle, who spoke these words so gayly, did not look as if she had spent much time in rebelling against her fate. Her tanned face may have been somewhat wrinkled for her forty-seven years, but they were pleasant wrinkles; her eyes were alive, her hair thick and brown, her teeth (they were her own) seemed good in spite of the dark rim of snuff around them, and her body was active looking. She sat perfectly relaxed, rocking gently back and forth and occasionally leaning over the front porch banisters to spit. The red voile dress she wore without a belt, for coolness, and she did not have on stockings; on her feet were faded blue felt bedroom slippers.

When she was about ten years old, Alice's father had moved his family of four children from the farm in Alamance County to Concord. Alice didn't go to school in Concord because she didn't have to and "there weren't no school buildings here the way there is now." And so when she was ten, she began to work in the mill.

"Yessir, when I started down here to plant No. 1, I was so little I had to stand on a box to reach my work. I was a spinner at first, then I learned to spool. When they put in them new winding machines, I asked them to learn me how to work 'em and they did. If I'd-a-been a man no telling how far I'd-a gone. It was mighty convenient for 'em— having a hand that could do all three, but I got mad and quit. In them days there was an agreement here in the mills that if a hand was to quit one, then the other mills in town wouldn't hire him, so I went over to Albemarle and I got me a job in the knitting mills..."

Then she went on to tell me of her marriage in Albemarle, of the birth of her two children there, and the death of her husband when Ruby, her oldest child, was "three year and three days old." She was more interested, though, in telling of how she learned to work a machine in the knitting mill in one day. "One day the boss man told me the hand that worked the machine that knit stockings was quittin', and he told me to go watch her to see if I couldn't learn it. Well, I stood right close by that hand all day and I watched 'er, so that the next day when she didn't come I was able to work the machine by myself."

After the death of her husband, Alice moved back to Concord and again went to work for the Cannon Mills. "I've worked for the Cannon Mills now for over thirty years," she announced proudly...

At present Alice works in the spinning room. There are only women in this division and she says they have a time together, talking, laughing and cutting up. "The section head don't hardly ever come around. Sometimes I tell him that us old widow women back there could go off to South Carolina to get married and come back again, but he wouldn't even know we'd been gone." When asked why men didn't work in the spinning room, she shrugged and made some remark about the patience and skill required for such work and added "you know how men are..." in a pitying tone.

The morning shift, on which Alice works, goes from 7:00 to 3:30, with a half an hour off for lunch. For two full weeks' work of five days a week she receives $31.00. When she lived over in another village (owned by the same company) her rent was $6.00 a month; now she lives with her daughter's family and contributes to their expenses...

Credit: Library of Congress, Manuscript Division, WPA Federal Writers' Project Collection

The Thchankats are shepherds of Landes, France, a race who passed their lives on stilts, crossing rivers and forests full of venomous snakes without danger. They have now almost died out, and Sylvain Dornon, whose portrait we give, is one of the last of the tribe. He made himself notorious by walking from his native village to Paris on his stilts, and even ascending the Eiffel Tower on those wooden supports. Thence he set off to walk to Moscow and back on his stilts. The Tchankats carry a pole, by which they elevate themselves on their stilts, and which makes a sort of third leg when they wish to rest.

Credit: Picture Collection, The Branch Libraries, The New York Public Library, Astor, Lenox and Tilden Foundations

The last of the Tchankats—Sylvain Dornon knitting on his stilts, 1893. Unknown photographer.

Knitting Through...
Unemployment

THE RISING TIDE
BY AMY HOLMAN

As the summer of 2003 waned, I lost my job in Manhattan, saw my frolicsome dog become feeble, got an agent to represent my nonfiction, taught at a writer's conference in Vermont, was hired to teach a three-week class at a university the following summer, and joined a knitting circle in my Brooklyn neighborhood. My general state was fragile and furious, mixed with feelings of concern and hope. I thought learning to knit would be creative and industrious, something to engage me with the outside world aside from walking my dog, and give me one regular appointment each week until I found a job.

The large, purple-painted Knitting Hands yarn shop down on Atlantic Avenue had a big front window draped with strings and soft balls of sensuous yarn, next to an ivory cabled poncho with sleeves. It had escaped my notice as a working woman, but it was inviting me inside when I went on an errand one hot August day. There, I joined a knitting circle instead of a class because I like to work at my own pace, I benefit from being around people at different stages of learning, and I wouldn't have to worry about making up a missed session. The Friday afternoon session was taught

75

by Barbara Kerr, a retired social worker who had been knitting since she was seventeen years old. Barbara lived with her husband on a houseboat that was docked in Sheepshead Bay. She traveled to conferences to teach color workshops and strip knitting—which is not like strip poker. (Wouldn't that be a deconstruction to strip down whenever you made a pattern mistake, and then dress in the irregular garment when you were done?) One woman in the class was advanced and learned how to knit delicate flowers for infant shoes and ruffles for infant sweaters. The rest of us were beginners.

The job search was fruitless, and the book proposal I submitted to my agent had to be rewritten before it could be sent out to editors. My goofy dog, who used to sail in front of me like a low-flying kite, now tiptoed behind me in arthritic dismay. Also, I had to knit a sampler of different stitches in a light-colored, basic wool before I could attempt a single project in any of the extravagant yarn skeins spilling out of the cubby holes of Knitting Hands. All advancement was delayed.

As autumn began to wax, my agent sent my proposal to eleven editors; a writers' group in Putnam County hired me as their guest poet; a minor character in *The Lost Garden,* a melancholy novel I was reading, turned out to be a knitting soldier in WWII who sent beautiful sweaters home to his fiancée; and state employees at the mandatory unemployment workshops I attended with fifty other discouraged adults at the Department of Labor a few blocks southeast of Knitting Hands dubiously tried to buck up our spirits by telling us that we were not alone—so many were unemployed, or about to be.

Knitting has stitches and patterns and textures and colors that mix and mingle. Once the stitch is understood, it's just a rhythm you can follow. Knitting a scarf ordered my mind when I had trouble rewriting a proposal for a book on how to get published so that I could return to it refreshed and flowing. The repetitive stitches are especially useful when thinking structurally, as for the chapter outline for the book. My topic, teaching writers to be detectives by following the publishing trails of their favorite writers, has many connections, but only one effective strategy that leads to success in publishing. Yet, the material had to be arranged differently for readers on the page than students in a classroom. It was only while knitting a fixed pattern of a checkerboard with a multihued Noro silk/wool that changed from bright jade through evergreen, olive, and stony brook to purple that my thoughts unwound and released my writer's block.

Barbara offered to teach me how to knit socks on two circular needles on a Saturday on her houseboat if I would help her with a pattern book proposal, and I accepted. It was a beautiful autumn day, and I took two subways to Sheepshead Bay, where Barbara's husband met me and drove me to the port. We walked along a dock to board the boat, I got the tour of upstairs and down, saw the place where her children had slept that was now yarn storage, enjoyed some lunch and good conversation, and examined intricate tin sculptures of a ship and a wacky train engine her husband had built. We worked on Barbara's pitch for the book, and then she got me started on the socks. Barbara had a computer program that enabled her to design a sock pattern specifically for my foot measurements; I'd brought two size 2 circular needles and bright, primary-colored sock yarn. The stitches were tiny and the technique strange at first, but I slowly caught on to it. As we knit and talked, we sat on a futon in the stern of the houseboat and listened to music from Barbara's new Bose radio. It was the sunniest fall day, and I thought about how lucky I was to have found such artistic kinship at a cast-off time in my working life.

Back in the circle, I began a cabled wool vest using a pattern from the '70s. It was a preppy sort of garment that I chose to alter using a wool that was dyed shades of dark green with a bit of ochre. Barbara taught me how to knit backwards out of the misplaced cable. I ran into trouble with the vest as snowstorms and holidays postponed the circle, so I set it aside in favor of gift scarves. At the same time, my house became the temporary home for a friend's two-year-old female German shepherd, which brought out in my old male dog one of the less publicized emotions of golden retrievers—outrage. Barbara retired from working at the store, and interim teachers substituted. They offered alternate viewpoints and attitudes. One was bossy and tactless, but showed us lovely stitch patterns, like the double moss stitch, which looked like little shells in the sweater she wore. The second replacement, Eve, had learned to knit at five years old and worked for years as a sample knitter before taking a job with a major clothing designer to save her wrists from carpal tunnel syndrome. She wore neutral colors, offered in her soft voice less complicated fixes to knitting mistakes, and had a serene presence. I admitted to her, with guilt, that I had investigated other yarn stores in Manhattan because they all had different yarn selections. It was the same way that I enjoyed many independent bookstores for their staff picks. Eve responded casually by saying that the interest every knitter had in exploring was beneficial to all merchants, but the way she said it was philosophical: The rising tide lifts all boats.

I unraveled and knit, again, unraveled and knit, again; when problems arose, I found patience where I'd never suspect. My dog was upset by the new dog's claim on his territory, which was me, and the new dog considered him her territory to guard, apparently from me, and both were jealous of the attention I managed to give either. While the proposal wasn't selling, an editor asked me to write a different book on artist colonies, and I finished the vest that was too short for my long torso. I started a new proposal, took on freelance work, bought beautiful yarn without projects in mind, and experimented with Fair Isle and lace.

Knitting is connection, the unraveling of yarn to pull loops through loops to create one fabric. I renewed my place in the circle every six weeks until the following summer because I liked the knitting community I found there—Tracy, Beth, Johanna, Flavia, Seeta, who managed the store, and Wendy, our last leader, who was just as loopy as we. Wendy shared the lore, industry, and trick of knitting. She told us about fishermen knitting at sea, belts fashioned for one-handed knitting, and how to twist stitches without a cable needle. We talked about sex, politics, children, fashion, and work. We had great ideas: bikini, poncho, suit, coat. Johanna's poncho was a success, with stripes of different-textured yarns in beige, brown, and sand, both fuzzy and silky. Tracy's lime-green bikini was well on the way to bind off when she met a new guy. Beth, who knit scarves and hats out of dark, reasonable wools, proved to be great at matching person, project, and yarn. I dream big and don't plan well, then see that planning might work along with the dreams.

The editor refused the proposal she requested, and my agent sent it to a new round of editors without missing a stitch. No full-time work arrived, the sweet and frustrated shepherd destroyed my mattress, my carefree golden refused to go in the yard that was more his than mine and was now becoming hers, and all the sweaters I tried knitting were too wide. I was hired for publishing consultations, small teaching jobs, and at last grasped circular knitting. It is good to take wild imagination down a practical notch and despair up into creative repair. My garments were often irregular, but my compatriots cheered.

Seeta took over the store and renamed it Knit-A-Way, and an editor liked the new proposal, asked for changes, and bought it as a book on MFA programs, colonies, and grants. I stopped the circle and let it twirl through my psyche. The German shepherd I now loved went home to my friend, and my golden acted bereft of her and then happily reclaimed me. Wearing my successful lacy sweaters, I continue to board all the nearby boats—Knit-A-Way, Brooklyn General, Purl Soho, The Point—that had risen on this fashionable knitting tide. I was unraveling when I started to knit, vulnerable and uncertain of my future, and found in the act and art of it connection and regeneration. Or, things had been the worst they could be and now they were worsted.

Excerpts from an interview at
Abyssinia Baptist Church—
Unemployed Section
and Adult Education

By Vivian Morris
May 2, 1939

"Reverend Powell* might be a Baptist preacher, but he sho don't believe only in preachin' bout God. He preached the Government right into givin' us all these teachers to teach us all the things we didn't have a chance to learn when we were young. This was the community house, but now it's a school, better for the community.

I do part time housework, in the afternoon.

Come to school every morning.

Comin' to school three years now.

Can't make my madam know, she'll think I'm getting' too smart.

I don't work Sundays.

I sing in the Choir...

You learn to sing here too, and sew, and knit, and type, and a whole lot of other things.

This one is good, I want to learn it soon.

I forgot the name, the Supervisor calls it by, oh yes Speech Improvement.

You know what that is?

Makes you talk better eh?

I'm gonna take it, soon as I git thew the knitting class.

Knitting is alright, but talking is better.

Nowadays you gotta talk yourself in and out of a lotta things.

If you want a job you gotta be able to talk the boss into givin' it to you. Then after you git it you gotta talk him into keepin' you...

If Reverend Powell couldn't do a lotta talking, dam if we'd have this center here.

The Government ain't givin' you nuthin so easy...

Education, Education, keep fightin' for it.

Reverend Powell prays, but he fights too, prayin' alone ain't gonna get you nowhere.

Sometimes when he prays, sounds like he's fightin' with God, but he's fightin' for all of us.

Now he's fightin' for jobs.

World's Fair jobs... Fifty jobs at the World's Fair, how'd we get 'em? Picketin', not prayin'...

Those girls in that picket line in front a Kress are students.

They're hungry.

We're all Hungry."

Credit: Library of Congress, Manuscript Division, WPA Federal Writers' Project Collection

* *During the Depression years, Adam Clayton Powell, Jr. became a prominent civil rights leader in Harlem, a predominantly black neighborhood in New York City. He organized mass meetings, rent strikes and public campaigns, forcing companies, utilities, and the 1939 World's Fair—like other fairs of its ilk in that era, notorious for discrimination against African Americans—to hire black employees. In 1937, he succeeded his father as pastor of Abyssinian Baptist Church. He then went on to serve eleven consecutive terms as Congressman from New York.*

"In the fall of 1864, Sojourner Truth traveled to Washington, D.C. to work in refugee camps set up by the government to administer to the freed people escaping the ravages of the Civil War. She taught sewing, knitting, and cooking, and gave speeches in which she exhorted the freed people to 'learn to be independent—learn industry and economy—and above all strive to show the people that they could be something.' This plain talk, along with admonitions not to live 'off the government,' got her thrown out of at least one gathering of freed people."

Credit: This Far By Faith *series, "1866–1945: from Emancipation to Jim Crow*
Sojourner Truth: A Promised Land for the Exodusters"
http://www.pbs.org/thisfarbyfaith/journey_3/p_5.html

Opposite: Sojourner Truth, three-quarter length portrait, seated at table with knitting, facing front. "I sell the shadow to support the substance." 1864. Unknown photographer.
Credit: Library of Congress Prints & Photographs Division, Gladstone Collection, reproduction #LC-DIG-ppmsca-08978

Knitting Through...
Politics

KNITTING THROUGH RED STATES VS. BLUE STATES
BY ERICA PEARSON

I learned how to knit right before the 2004 presidential election. As a lifelong crafts junkie, I had always thought of myself as a potential knitter, but just hadn't taken the important step of actually learning. After I had mentioned that I wanted to learn to knit one time too many, my knitter friends finally stepped in. One bought me needles and yarn, while the other sat patiently next to me on the couch for hours to coach me through each row. I didn't realize it then, but their timing was spot on. When November 2 arrived, knitting and purling—still new to me then, the stitches just beginning to fall into a rhythm of their own—got me through a very long night.

I was working as an editor at a free daily newspaper with a bare-bones staff and a budget to match. Unlike *The New York Times* and even most newspapers, we didn't have a small army of correspondents at polling places around the country and a crowded newsroom humming late into election night. Just four of us were scheduled to stay until a winner was declared: our editor-in-chief, a reporter, a photo editor, and me.

I was in the middle of my first project: a simple stockinette-stitch scarf in black with a red stripe on each end. It was for my husband, who wasn't likely to wear something unless it was red, black, some combination of the two, or had skulls on it. At this point, skulls were definitely out of my league. Learning how to put in the first red stripe had been enough of a challenge. My friend had set me up with several skeins of Bulky Lamb's Pride and a pair of size 10 bamboo needles. At first, it was difficult for me to keep the yarn firmly and evenly wrapped around the needles, especially at the end of each row. Soon, I started to feel comfortable with the feel of the wool sliding through my fingers and the weight and grip of the bamboo. The saleswoman at Downtown Yarns had given my friend excellent advice: This combination of yarn and needles was perfect for a new knitter's first scarf.

I hadn't yet broken out the knitting at work. Most days, I was too busy to even think about it, and it didn't quite feel like a public activity at that point. I was just getting used to keeping my elbows in and finishing a few rows on the subway without gouging the person sitting next to me. But as that Tuesday turned into night—and those early exit polls that pointed to a John Kerry victory changed into votes tallied for George W. Bush—my fingers started itching to pick up the needles. I needed something to do besides obsessively checking the Associated Press newswire for results. I thought that the constant motion and concentration of knitting might somehow absorb some of my nervous energy. All journalistic objectivity aside, there was something about the possibility of keeping on Dubya as commander-in-chief that made me a little sick to my stomach.

The Associated Press began calling states around 7:00 PM: Georgia, Indiana, and Kentucky went for Bush, and

Vermont for Kerry. We kept checking the wires for updates and shuffling between television channels. I decided to take out the scarf and pour some of my anxiety into the yarn. Not only did I care personally about the election's outcome—and what it meant for the country's future—but I knew that the later the returns came in, the more difficult things would be at the office. What would we put on the front page if the results were unclear? But the rhythm of knitting those twenty stitches, then purling back through them, then holding up the scarf to see how long it was and if there were any mistakes, then wondering if my husband would actually wear it when I finished, helped me to relax.

Also, if there was nothing to do but wait, at least I could be productive. As 8:00 PM approached, I started to pick up speed. I ignored the wisecracks and requests for knitted Speedos from my colleagues. I was actually getting better at this and didn't have to think so much about just keeping the yarn on the needles. I began to wonder about what I would knit next, once this scarf and this night were over. Row after row, the scarf grew, at a seemingly faster pace than the results came in. Kerry won Delaware, Connecticut, Washington, D.C., Illinois, Maine, Maryland, New Jersey, and Massachusetts, the AP declared. Alabama, Oklahoma, Tennessee, and West Virginia went for Bush. I looked over the scarf and thought I could see the row where I finally began to lock into an even gauge; the little black Vs were all lined up and uniform.

As the ball of yarn dwindled, I wrapped the scarf around my neck to keep it from the floor as I knit at my desk. It was past 11:00 PM now. Arkansas, Kansas, Nebraska, North Dakota, South Dakota, Texas, Wyoming, South Carolina, North Carolina, Virginia, Louisiana, and Mississippi for Bush. Knit one row, purl one row. New York and Rhode Island for Kerry. The country's map took form in red and blue. Pennsylvania and California to Kerry; Arizona, Idaho, and Missouri for Bush. I wondered how many other people around the country were sitting in front of televisions with their knitting needles moving. I wondered what results they were hoping to hear. A red-and-blue striped scarf was really the appropriate project for the evening, I thought. You could even plan it so that the stripes were thick for some states and thin for others, like the large swaths of color on the map that the television commentators kept pointing to.

When midnight struck, Florida was declared for Bush. It seemed that the whole election would all come down to Ohio, as Kerry later took Michigan, Hawaii, New Hampshire, Oregon, Washington, and Minnesota, and Bush won Nevada, Colorado, Montana, and Utah. On CBS, Dan Rather was making the four of us in the office laugh, saying, "Ohio becomes like a sauna for the two candidates. All they can do is wait and sweat," and perhaps my favorite, "This situation in Ohio would give aspirin a headache." I looked down at my knitting and realized that it had grown even longer than I realized. I was able to notice the bit of mohair blended into the Lamb's Pride; it stood out under the office's fluorescent lights. I started to think that I just might finish the scarf before our president-elect was declared.

At 3:00 AM, NBC reported that Kerry had gone to bed. As it grew later and later, Iowa, Wisconsin, New Mexico, and Ohio were still up in the air, and in the office, we struggled with a too-close-to-call front page. NBC and Fox projected that Ohio would go to Bush, but that wasn't enough for us to go on. If we waited much longer, it would be too late for our presses to finish printing in time to get papers on the street for the morning commute. So we decided to hedge it and call the race "A Squeaker" on the front page to let readers know that a president-elect had not been declared when we went to press. Finally, I had to put down the needles and get to work on editing the latest wire story, even though I had maybe ten rows to go before putting in the second red stripe.

I had to finish my scarf the next day. By then, Kerry had conceded. I was too tired to knit as I rode the subway back to the office. Work went by in a blur, amid talk of a nation divided. After the uncertainty of the night before, Thursday's front page headline, "Dubya Does It," was easier to come up with, but I was having my own trouble coming to terms with the news.

As soon as I got home that night, I took out the scarf and finished its final rows. Once I bound off, I knew I should feel a greater sense of accomplishment—I had actually finished my first knitting project. But as I looked over my work, I could see a spot at the scarf's very beginning where I'd dropped a stitch only to pick it up again a few rows later, leaving a little hole. The hole had been there all along, but I hadn't noticed it; the black yarn was pretty good at camouflaging mistakes.

At first I thought it didn't matter. My husband, with the scarf around his neck, said it didn't matter. Then I decided it mattered too much. Holding up the scarf and saying, "I was knitting this when Bush re-took the White House," didn't seem so appealing. I told my husband that I would remake the scarf; it would be just as long, but ribbed so it wouldn't curl under so much.

As I unraveled the fabric, unzipping each row, I thought about the moments in which each stitch took form. I hadn't really understood the phrase "a stitch in time," before, but it made perfect sense to me as I turned the scarf that had taken me more than a night to knit back into a ball of yarn. Of course, the events of the day and night before couldn't be undone so easily.

Beginner's Scarf
(a.k.a. Election Night Scarf Redux)
by Erica Pearson

Yarn:
2 skeins Brown Sheep Company Lamb's Pride Bulky
    (125 yards) in Onyx
1 skein Brown Sheep Company Lamb's Pride Bulky
    (125 yards) in Ruby Red
Needles:
1 pair size 10½ US

With black yarn, cast on 25 stitches.
Row 1: Knit 1, purl 1, repeat until last stitch, knit 1.
Row 2: Purl 1, knit 1, repeat until last stitch, purl 1.
Work in this 1 x 1 rib pattern for 8 more rows. Join red
    yarn and work in rib for 4 rows (don't cut the black yarn,
    twist it with the red at the beginning of the third row so
    you are ready pick it up again at the end of the red
    stripe).
Cut red yarn, leaving enough of a tail to weave in later, and
    work with black in rib pattern until scarf is 4 inches from
    desired length.
Work 4 rows in red as in beginning of scarf, cut red yarn
    and work with black for 10 rows.
Bind off loosely in rib pattern and weave in ends.

Knitting Through It

Four letters to Abraham Lincoln

Adams Jeff Co., NY, March 4th, 1861

Sir this pair of Gloves was knit Expressly as a present to your excellency by Mrs. Lucy A. Thomas, widow & relict of the late Hon. Ira Thomas of Adams Jeff Co. N. Y.

This lady will be 80 years of age April 8th 1861.

They are presented accompanied by her best respects to Mrs. Lincoln, and also by her prayers for the success and prosperity of the Government under your Excellency's administration.

Her Sons and relatives constituting no small portion of the population of Adams, are all zealous Republicans of the old Whig Stamp, and are all rejoiced at the success of their votes, which have aided in Elevating to the highest office in the Gift of the American People The Man, who if not first in war or in peace, is truly at the present time first in the hearts of his Countrymen.

Lucy A. Thomas

Ft. Howard, January 11th, 1864

Dear President Lincoln

please excuse the freedom I use in encroaching upon your time for a moment, and also accept the emblem of our Countrys Freedom which accompanies this note, from one that greatly admires the Fidelity—Patriotism, and Wisdom, which you have manifested throughout this wicked and terible Rebellion, I send it to you with the sincere hope that our great banner may soon wave over every foot of this great republic and over a freed and happy People, and I believe you are destined through Providence to guide the great Ship of State safely through this Storm into the Harbor of peace and Freedom, therefore I hope you may be sustained by grace and live to be our next President (no very enviable position I should judge at present however).

your sincere friend

Mrs H S Crocker

PS the scarf is some of my own knitting and inventing. I tried to knit a Spread Eagle over your name but did not succeed—

H S C

Groton, NH, January 1865

Dear Sir

Please allow an oald Ladey of ninty One years of age to presnt you a very humble testimoney of esteeme & confidence in the shape of a pair of socks knit with my own hands & allow me to say that I remember the tryals pased thrugh in revoulition days. I lost two Brothers out of three that was in the servis of the cuntery. besides Uncles & a number of cousins. & my prayer to Him that doethe all things well, that holdethe this nation in the hollow of His hand & hath continued my life to this time, & has Enabled me to worke almost dailey from the commcmnt of this rebelion to the present hour for the soldiers (God bless them) that you might be richley indoued with that wisdom which you have so much kneaded to enable you to bare so grate responsibilities & to do that that is for the good of our bleding Country & I do pray that you may live to see this rebelion ended & with it slavery (which I do abomonate) wiped from our land, & long thereafter to witness & Enjoy the fruits of your labour—you will pardon this intrusion upon your time & beleive me your to be your frind & freind of my bleding countery; Sarah Phelps.

Groton. N. H. Jany. 1865 .

Salem, MA, February 7th, 1865.

A year or two since, a pair of socks was sent to you from Mrs. Abner Bartlett, of Medford, Mass., which you kindly acknowledged. She was 87 years old on the 24th of Dec. 1864.—and has knit more than three hundred pairs of socks for the soldiers since Sept. 1861. She has consented to have me send the 300th pair to you as a birth-day gift.

Mrs. Bartlett is the only surviving sister of Tristam Burges, formerly in Congress from Rhode Island; and, although so far advanced in years, no one is more alive to the great issues of the hour, or more inspired to a true love of liberty,—and no one could have a firmer confidence in yourself or cherish a more unwavering faith in the perfect triumph of her Country's cause.

With the highest respect,

I am faithfully yours.

Geo. W. Briggs.

Credit: Abraham Lincoln Papers at the Library of Congress, Manuscript Division (Washington, D.C.: American Memory Project, [2000–02]), http://memory.loc.gov/ammem/ alhtml/alhome.html, accessed November 2006. Transcribed and annotated by the Lincoln Studies Center, Knox College, Galesburg, Illinois.

As Anne Macdonald maintains in her book, *No Idle Hands*, after the various war-knitting bees of World War II, American knitters were pretty much knitted out. Yarn companies worked diligently to recapture interest in what was coming to be seen as a craft for "grannies," with little initial success.

"Young women of the 1920s rejected knitting as 'women's work,'" according to a 2005 article in *The New York Times* by Carol E. Lee. "The industry worked hard to win them over with new yarn colors, knitting marathons, and contests offering sizeable prizes. Grace Coolidge, then the first lady, even joined knitting contests to help generate interest."

Sources: No Idle Hands, *Anne L. Macdonald, Ballantine Books New York, 1988. pp. 242–243*
"A Pastime of Grandma and the 'Golden Girls' Evolves into a Hip Hobby" by Carol E. Lee, The New York Times, *March 30, 2005*

Opposite: Grace Coolidge, half-length portrait, seated, knitting, facing left. By Herbert E. French, August 6, 1923.
Credit: Library of Congress, Prints & Photographs Division, National Photo Company Collection, reproduction #LC-USZ62-131581

Knitting Through... Prison

BELIEFS & CUSTOMS—FOLKSTUFF;
SOCIAL CUSTOMS OF THE PAST

EXCERPTS FROM AN INTERVIEW WITH
MRS. I. E. DOANE,
BEAUFORT COUNTY, SOUTH CAROLINA
BY CHLOTILDE R. MARTIN

Mrs. I. E. Doane of Beaufort, who is eighty-one years old, gives an interesting picture of life in the Lowcountry of South Carolina during the Civil War period.

Mr. Cummings owned only a few slaves and since slaves were expensive to own, he believed it to his advantage to treat them well in order to get the most interest out of his investment... Each family had its own cabin, furnished with beds, tables, benches and other assistance of her daughters' and the slave women. When the cloth was made she cut the garments and gave them to the slave mothers to sew under her direction... They were not taught to read and write but were given religious instruction on Sunday afternoons, when the mistress usually read the Bible and talked to them... The children of the slaves played with the white children of the house and many a good time they had, too, Mrs. Doane recalls.

Mrs. Doane remembers her father coming home from the war, six months after the conflict had ended. He had been in prison, and had to walk all the way home from the prison camp. She remembers that he would not come into the house until he had washed and changed . . . as he was covered with vermin. She recalls hearing him tell of a profitable little trading business he had developed while in prison. His initial stock consisted of some knitted gloves, socks and other articles, which his wife had sent him. It had been very cold that winter and these warm articles of clothing were in great demand. Her father's brother had been killed during a battle in Virginia. The flag had been shot down and he was the third man killed while attempting to run it up again.

Credit: Library of Congress, Manuscript Division, WPA Federal Writers' Project Collection

1,200 HATS: ART AND HEALING IN THE MAKING
BY SHERRI WOOD

From September 2002 to September 2003, I was a weekly volunteer at the North Carolina Correctional Institution for Women (NCCIW). My role was simple: I was an umbilical cord to the outside world. I didn't have to do anything but show up and sit with the women. We spent our Tuesday afternoons drawing, talking, sometimes reading, and eventually crocheting. This is the story of how the practice of craft can heal and how the process of healing can become art.

I met with a revolving group of about thirty-five women who were a part of a prison reform program called the Last Alternative Therapeutic Community of Hope (LATCH). The purpose of LATCH was to allow incarcerated women the opportunity to work on their emotional healing while doing their time. They would strive to develop healthy interpersonal skills through socialization within the bounds of a supportive and therapeutic peer community. They were a "close knit" group, so to speak . . . BUT they weren't allowed to knit! Knitting needles were considered dangerous—potential weapons—by the prison authority. Plastic crochet hooks were the only craft implements allowed, and crochet was the only craft the women were able to perform unsupervised.

Many of the women crocheted as a way to pass the tediousness of time, to meditate on future possibilities, or to reflect on the past. They made gifts for one another and for people they knew on the outside because each incarcerated woman was allowed only up to two handmade objects as personal property. Usually they made blankets, hats, or bizarre, colorful dolls—each about the size of a six-month-old infant—stuffed with plastic bags. They made these dolls for fellow inmates who had to leave their young children behind, on the outside. The dolls served, not as replacements for their children, but as transitional objects that helped the women retain a sense of connection to their families during their incarceration. For most of the women, separation from their children was often the most painful reality of being in prison.

Volunteers were not allowed to give or do any one thing to or for any one person if we couldn't do it for every person in the prison, so the answer in prison is always NO.

"Can I keep this pen?"

"Do you have a stamp?"

"Could you mail this letter for me?"

"No!" I answered. "There is a rule that says I can't . . . give you the pen, or a stamp, or mail your letter."

As a way of focusing the creative energy of our weekly crochet sessions, the women and I looked for ways to say YES in prison. One day, we came upon the idea of crocheting 1,200 hats. One colorful, unique hat for every woman incarcerated at NCCIW. This was a perfectly subversive yet appropriate way for us to say, "Yes!"

A call went out in the bulletin of the United Church of Chapel Hill, inviting members of the congregation to unburden themselves of the guilt of unfinished projects. Like loaves and fishes, bundles of yarn that had been hidden in closets (remnants from the gifts of sweaters, afghans, mittens, etc.) were gathered and given to the "guilty" for transformation. Over $7,000 worth of yarn was collected by the membership. Additionally, women in the church crocheted hats for our project on Sunday mornings to show their solidarity for the women at NCCIW.

With this new focus, our weekly meetings evolved into three-hour "Stitch & Bitch" or, to coin a new phrase for this age-old tradition, "Make & Partake" sessions. We didn't use patterns to crochet the hats, but found our way through improvisation. Those who knew how to crochet taught those who wanted to learn. People who didn't want to crochet drew or wrote, documenting our meetings through images and words. We were united through our creative goal and we shared our lives in the process.

Today I started on another hat. It is black and yellow. Then I will help someone else. Some of my sisters are journaling and helping people. Ms. Sherri is teaching Ms. Vance and Ms. Jones to make a hat. Another sister is making her own project which is a blanket. Now she is working on a red hat. Ms. McMillan is doing strings so we can hang them from the ceiling. Ms. V. Matson is laughing at Ms. Jenkins cause she is acting crazy. Ms. Deer is making something, I don't know what she's making but she's making something. Ms. Willis just got discouraged and had to break her hat down. Now she working it out. Ms. Meredith is assisting. Ms. Lochlan is making sure everyone is doing the right stitch.
—Claudia, report from NCCIW, January 28, 2003

The LATCH women embraced the project and easily related the making and giving of the hats to their therapeutic work. Our hope was to create a gift exchange that crisscrossed the boundary of the prison walls. First, the donated yarn came into the prison, then the hats went out in the form of an exhibition. The hats served as a witness, speaking through the absence of the 1,200 incarcerated women, many of whom were mothers.

I recently learned to knit and have been making a few hats. I like knitting on the bus, by myself or with friends. It makes me feel connected to a tradition of crafty women & I feel connected to the women who made these hats.
—Kelly, visitor comment

I was able to appreciate what the hats represented: the number of women incarcerated in our state who are normally unable to make their voices heard. I was able to imagine the hands that had made the hats and the different women who belonged to the hands. I also wondered what each hat would say if it could tell the story of its creator.
—Carmen Crompton, visitor comment

I am really speechless, but my eyes are wet. I came to see the "Hats" with my three-year-old. All I could think about was how these women couldn't be with their kids (no matter the reason for their being behind bars). The delicate nature of these "Hats" shows/reveals a lot about how they feel about their families and children.
—Leoneda Inge-Barry, visitor comment

As you look at "1,200 Hats" and think of the people who crafted them, you don't think of crime, you don't think of violence, you don't think of hate. You think of pride, and of hope. And with each glance of hope you see despair; with each glance of pride you see humility; with each glance of freedom you see a person in prison, and at that point it no longer seems to matter why. You wish for each hat to be free, and hope that each hat's maker can find freedom.
—William Roberson, visitor comment

After the public exhibition, we envisioned the hats being redistributed to the general population at NCCIW. We thought of offering a hat as a gift or talisman, to ease the transformation for the newly incarcerated during intake. Unfortunately, this was vetoed by the warden "for reasons of security"—no further explanation was given.

One day, a LATCH woman came to one of our Tuesday sessions wearing a purple and white crocheted hat with a butterfly embroidered on its band. She told me her mother had made it for her. She hadn't seen her mother since she was a child; now they were reunited in prison! After some debate, the LATCH women chose to donate the hats they made to the Mother/Child Prison Reform Initiative. This initiative was designed to break the intergenerational cycle of crime, poverty, substance abuse, and domestic violence by allowing nonviolent women offenders with children under twelve to serve their sentences with their children at an alternative facility called Summit House. The hats were auctioned and the money raised went to this program, which the women felt directly benefited their sisters and their families.

So much of what has gone wrong in our lives began with the break-up of our families. To have a hand in any project that aims to hold families—mothers and their children—together, is a way for me to rebuild what I have destroyed, and hopefully keep another from starting down that empty broken road. This is my contribution to Hope and to Healing."
—Patricia, hat maker, NCCIW

I started making hats to support others and, to my surprise, I received the gift of freedom to create.
—Beverly Sanders, hat maker, United Church

Reflecting on all the twists and turns of the project, it is clear that the installation of the hats, however moving to those on the outside, was not the heart of the art but the by-product. The art was in the making of the hats. Healing came from the experience of recognizing our relationships to each other through our shared brokenness, through the purgatory of our personal prisons, and through our hopes for being better. We all came to know that the external practice of making something together—of crocheting (or knitting) for others—has the power to mirror, communicate, connect, and transform the internal realities of those who partake.

Postscript. The installation included portraits by photographer Artie Dixon of some of the hat makers, along with the hats they made for the project. Artie made portraits of both the women incarcerated at NCCIW and the women of the

United Church of Chapel Hill who crocheted in solidarity with their sisters in prison. The photographs point to the similarities between the "guilty" and the "innocent" rather than our differences.

Although the hats were auctioned to the privileged, the crocheted chains, made by women at NCCIW to hang the hats, still exist. Now in the form of a 50-foot barrier/curtain that resides in my studio and that I've exhibited on several occasions, this remnant continues to live on the outside as a witness to the fact that more than 1,200 women continue to live on the inside, in the largest correctional facility in the state of North Carolina.

A version of this essay originally appeared in KnitKnit #5, *May 2005.*

CROCHETED HAT BY SHERRI WOOD
The hats made by the residents of the North Carolina Correctional Institution for Women were crocheted improvisationally, without a pattern, so each is unique. But they are easy to replicate:

Start with a small ring of chain stitches—this will be the top of the hat. Single crochet for one round.

"1,200 Hats," created by the residents of the North Carolina Correctional Institution for Women, on view at the Durham Art Guild, NC, 2003.
Credit: Sherri Wood, 2003

Continue to single crochet, or switch to double crochet, spiraling out from the center. Add stitches to increase, or double up on stitches, to create a bowl shape to fit the head of the intended wearer. When hat is almost the desired length, decrease or skip stitches to pull it in around the ears. Cast off.

Prisoners knitting in one of their classrooms, Sing Sing, c. 1915, Ossining, NY. Originally copyrighted by Underwood & Underwood. Unknown photographer.
Credit: Library of Congress, Prints and Photographs Division, reproduction #LC-USZ62-98906

The turn to the nineteenth century saw both men and women in prisons across the country knitting. Albion Correctional Facility supported a vocational program of "supervised housework" for its female inmates, which included knitting as well as cooking and table etiquette. Its stated mission was to give the women "such training in domestic work as will eventually enable them to find employment, secure good homes, and be self-supporting." Male prisoners at Sing Sing were taught to make most of their own clothing, including knitted garments; a *New York Times* pictorial from March 14, 1915, which unfortunately could not be reproduced here, depicted uniformed convicts, some of them draped in their own creations, knitting in the prison yard while the prison mandolin club performed a concert. Today, the behind-bars craft tradition continues, if the rationale for it differs from latter-day thinking. According to an article by Betty Christiansen for *Interweave Knits* in 2003, male prisoners at the Jackson Correctional Facility in Wisconsin make hats and blankets for charity, as a form of mandatory community service. Others, at the Limon Correctional Facility in Colorado, learn crocheting, machine knitting, and quilting as rehabilitative pastimes. Sherri Wood's essay, "1,200 Hats," on page 103, gives a deeper perspective on this topic.

Knitting Through...
War

ALL NEW YORK IN BIG KNITTING BEE

Seventh Avenue and Plaza Folk to
Toil in Central Park

Ye village knitting bee has descended upon New York. Gotham the proud has put on its specs and will mingle tout ensemble in a three days' festival of "catch and twist and over and catch." Central Park is to be the scene of this latest orgy of fashionable war work.

Whether or not the lion and the lamb are to lie down together on the lawn in order to make this millennial festival complete has not been announced. It is certain that Seventh Avenue and the Plaza are scheduled to click needles side by each and that socks for Doughboy Israelewitz will grow under the same spreading chestnut trees where a helmet for Colonel Claverly-Amsterdam is being done in silk and merino.

Democracy at its knitting will no doubt be photographed and feted to a fare-ye-well but the prospects are that the Yanks over there, who have failed to show any signs of cold feet to date, will not be allowed to get chilblains anywhere else, not even on their trigger fingers.

"Quantity production" is the aim of the knit-fest.

Credit: From the Stars and Stripes, *August 2, 1918, Vol. 1 No. 26*

EXCERPT FROM "NO NEWS FOR ME" BY
JOHN ROSS DIX
1864, FROM 500 ILLUSTRATED BALLADS,
LITHOGRAPHED AND PRINTED BY
CHARLES MAGNUS, NO. 12
FRANKFORT STREET, NEW YORK

No news for me—No news for me!
I wond'r where can Johnny be!
He told me he would surely write—I fear that he is
    fall'n in fight.

My little cot looks drear and lone
Since Johnny to the wars has gone—
The brook which sang so sweet a tune,
Now murmurs sadly to the moon;
And all day long I idly sit,
Or by my silent hearth I knit;
And tear-drops down my cheeks fall free,
Because there is no news for me!

Credit: Library of Congress, Rare Book and Special Collections Division, America Singing: Nineteenth-Century Song Sheets.

KNITTING IN TIMES OF WAR AND PEACE
BY VERA VIVANTE

I was fortunate to learn how to knit before the war in England, primarily because there was an abundance of wool in a variety of colors. In our town (and many others), there existed The Scotch Wool & Hosiery Shop. Polished wood molding framed large, bevel-glass windows where knit garments were attractively displayed to lure one inside to the luminous shelf-lined walls that were filled to the ceiling with wool. My mother and grandmother were constant knitters, and they made all our clothing—jerseys, pullovers, hats, gloves, socks, bathing suits. They sometimes even knitted our undergarments, vests, and knickers (in cotton), with a little pocket in which to keep a much-needed handkerchief secure.

It was 1937. Preparations for the coronation of King George VI had begun. Banners and streamers were everywhere in England, especially in London, where we lived. Their majestic glow and radiant colors seemed to be pulling the country out of the dull, austere Depression years. It was the appropriate time for me to *implore* my mother to let me knit a tea-cozy in two shades of green. Young as I was (eight years old), I realized this was asking for the moon. "We have no money for luxuries," was the expected reply. My sister, a few years older than me, was already knitting garments for herself. She had mastered cable stitch and a lace pattern in the shape of multiple leaves, which my envious eyes admired. Was it my downcast face or the cheerful festivities about us that prompted my mother to change her mind in those frugal times?

The tea-cozy pattern looked difficult because it had a padded effect to serve its purpose, but actually it was just the basic plain knit stitch on every row. The padding was achieved by crossing each color of the wool alternately behind the next ten stitches of the other color. This procedure carried each color along the row and made a ridge effect in the front that decreased toward the top so that the final look was something like a puffed-out cantaloupe cut in half. My grandmother joined the two sides together, which allowed space for spout and handle. She finished the detail-trim on top with crochet leaves and flowers. Of course, we all thought it was magnificent and stared at it for hours. Here was a solid piece of fabric made from a mere thread of wool on two straight needles by hands that had learnt the ancient "inter-looping" skill of knitting—a thrilling magical moment. Although it took months in the making, this first knitting adventure had thrust deep roots into my creative potential and led me further into its realm.

A desire to make dolls' clothes came next. The pictures in pattern books were cleverly enticing and irresistible. My father made a smaller pair of lightweight wooden needles for me to better handle the softer–quality wool required to knit bonnets and frocks. The soft wool (mostly left-over wool from clothing items) came in a wider variety of shades, an added attraction indeed for my newfound delight. My passion for knitting was firmly in place. I still feel a quiver of pleasure when thinking of those charming little garments.

Two years later, my world—the entire world—changed. On September 3, 1939, World War II was declared. The rationing of food and goods was immediately in effect. Men

A part of the Uintah and Ouray Indian Red Cross
Auxiliary, Fort Duchesne, Utah. Unknown photographer.
Portrait of sitting unidentified Native American Uinta (Ute)
women and a girl, Fort Duschesne, Utah.

The women, who are part of the Red Cross Auxiliary,
wear dresses and shawls and knit, 1918. *Credit: Denver
Public Library, Western History Collection, Call #30733*

Berlin—knitting for soldiers in doctor's anteroom. WWI (no date available). Unknown photographer.

Credit: Library of Congress, Prints & Photographs Division, George Grantham Bain Collection, Reproduction #LC-DIG-ggbain-18336

"During World War I and World War II, the American Red Cross launched nationwide, volunteer-driven knitting campaigns to supply soldiers and civilians with warm clothing. The participants belonged to a unit then called the Production Corps, which also produced bandages and sewn garments like pajamas for veteran's hospitals and civilians.

Military knitting patterns were designed to be compatible with soldier's and sailor's uniforms and were required to be knitted in olive drab or navy blue. There were also patterns that were designed for convalescing soldiers, such as the 'Walking Cast Toe Sock,' the 'Cap for Bandaged Head,' and the 'Man's Coat Sweater.'"

Source: http://www.redcross.org/museum/history/

As is evidenced by the two photos here, however, war knitting crossed lines both ethnic and political.

RED CROSS GLOVES

Reproduced with permission from the Canadian Red Cross

MATERIALS: 4 oz. Special Heavy Red Cross Service Yarn
Set of 4 No. 11 Steel Knitting Needles (points at both ends)
Colours: Khaki, Navy, Airforce

MEASUREMENTS: Width all around hand at thumb
8 ins.
Tension: 6 1/2 sts.=1 inch
Check your tension—see inside back cover.

RIGHT GLOVE: Cast on 48 sts. loosely (16, 16, 16).
Work 3 1/2 ins. ribbing (K2, P2). Knit 6 rounds plain
knitting. Proceed:

To make gusset for thumb: 1st round: P1. (Inc. 1 st. in
next st. K1) twice. P1. Knit to end of round *Next 2
rounds:** Knit, purling the sts. which were purled in
previous round. **4th round:** P1. Inc. 1 st. in next st. Knit
to the 2 sts. before the next purl st. Inc. 1 st. in next st.
K1. P1. Knit to end of round.* Repeat from * to * until
there are 16 sts. between the 2 purled sts. **Next 2 rounds:**
Knit, purling the sts. which were purled in previous
round. **Next round:** K1. Cast on 4 sts. Slip next 16 sts.
onto a thread and leave for thumb. Knit to end of round.
Knit 13 rounds. Proceed:

To make fingers: 1st finger: Knit first 4 sts. Slip all but
last 10 sts. onto thread. Cast on 2 sts. Knit last 10 sts.
Divide these 16 sts. on 3 needles. Join in round. Knit 3
ins. plain knitting.

Next round: (K2tog.) 8 times. Break wool. Thread end through remaining sts. Draw up and fasten securely. **Finish all fingers and thumb in same manner.**

2nd finger: Knit next 6 sts. of round. Cast on 2 sts. Knit last 6 sts. of round and pick up and knit 3 sts. at base of 1st. finger. Divide these 17 sts. on 3 needles. Knit 3-1/2 ins. **Next round:** (K2tog.) 8 times. K1.

3rd finger: Knit next 6 sts. of round. Cast on 2 sts. Knit last 6 sts. of round and pick up and knit 2 sts. at base of 2nd finger. Divide these 16 sts. on 3 needles. Knit 3 ins. **Next round:** (K2tog.) 8 times.

4th finger: Knit remaining sts. from thread. Pick up and knit 4 sts. at base of 3rd finger. Divide these 14 sts. on 3 needles. Knit 2-1/2 ins. **Next round:** (K2tog.) 7 times.

The Thumb: Knit the 16 sts. which were left for thumb, and pick up and knit 4 sts. at base of thumb. Divide these 20 sts. on 3 needles. **Next 2 rounds:** Knit, dec. twice over the 4 sts. which were picked up at base of thumb. (16 sts. in round). Knit 2-1/2 ins. **Next round:** (K2tog.) 8 times.

LEFT GLOVE: Work as given for Right Glove until fingers are reached. Proceed:

To make fingers: 1st finger: Knit first 14 sts. Slip remaining sts. onto a thread. Cast on 2 sts. Divide these 16 sts. on 3 needles. Join in round. Finish finger and work remainder of glove as given for Right Glove, beginning at back of glove to knit up sts. for remaining fingers.

Knitting Through... Poverty

Eliza blocking lace in the Oomingmak shop.
Credit: Dominic Cotignola, 2006

Knitting Softens the Impact as Worlds Collide
by Donna Druchunas

Note: The words Native and Outsider are capitalized in Alaska when referring to people or cultural traditions. The term Eskimo is used in Alaska to refer to the Native Alaskan people belonging to the Yup'ik, Cup'ik, St. Lawrence Island Yup'ik, and Inupiat groups. These people are related to the Inuit of Canada and are not Indians. There are also Indian tribes in Alaska, so the term Eskimo actually helps avoid confusion. The phrase Native Alaskan can refer to a specific group or refer to all of the indigenous people of the state as one larger group. Many people in the lower 48 think that Eskimo is a disrespectful term, but it is commonly used with respect in Alaska.
—DD

In Shishmaref, a grandmother stops knitting to examine the rows of salmon drying on her driftwood fish rack. Recently returned from summer fish camp, she and her husband must dry and store all of the season's catch before winter sets in.

In Unalakleet, a life-long knitter and author finishes writing an article for the Musk Ox Farm's newsletter, puts down her pen, and picks up her knitting. Outside, the wind groans as snow drifts in on the air currents from the nearby hills.

In St. Mary's, a young mother yells for her kids to turn down the sound on their X-box video game so she can concentrate on the intricate lace knitting chart she is working from. They come in and ask for a snack of *akutaq*, or Eskimo ice cream, to tide them over until supper, which will not be served until their father comes home from his job at the local school. She takes a break and whips together a treat made from seal oil, trout, and salmonberries.

In Anchorage, a middle-aged woman goes home from work, cooks dinner, and sits down to watch TV. Before she goes to bed, she knits half of a nachaq hood. During the night, she dreams of her mother and brother at home in Nightmute.

These women, and over 200 others scattered across the state of Alaska, have been knitting through cultural change for decades. As members of Oomingmak Musk Ox Producers' Co-operative, they knit feather-weight lace using qiviut (kiv'-ee-yoot), the wooly down of the musk ox. Their purpose can be summed up in two ideas: economic imperative and self determination.

Most knitters today don't knit to make money. We knit to express our creativity, to entertain ourselves, to make special gifts for our loved ones, and to relax. But all across rural Alaska, knitting is one of the few ways women can make money without abandoning their homes and traditional lifestyle.

I first learned of the Oomingmak knitters about six years ago when I read an article about the co-op in Piecework *magazine. I was so intrigued to learn about these women that I started on my own journey to learn about their lives, their culture, their knitting, and the qiviut yarn that they knit with. I read literally hundreds of books and magazine articles, spent untold hours surfing the web, and eventually found my way to Alaska to visit the knitters myself. Their story turned out to be more fascinating than I could ever have imagined and my adventure to Alaska changed my life more than I would have guessed.*

For tens of thousands of years, Eskimo peoples have inhabited the arctic and sub-arctic regions of Alaska. Many of the villages that are home to Yup'ik and Inupiat people today have been inhabited by their ancestors for thousands of years. These people never lived in the ice-igloos so often portrayed in cartoons and children's books. They built underground houses framed with driftwood or whale bones and covered them with sod. A tunnel below the ground level made a weatherproof entryway, and a single sealskin window in the roof let in the little sunlight available at the beginning and end of the dark, winter season. A large, central dwelling housed the men and older boys and served as a place for community gatherings and festivals, while smaller single-family dwellings were home to women, girls, and very young boys. Men hunted, and women took over once the animals were brought back to the village. Although they did not spin the fur from any of the animals taken in hunts, these women developed amazing skills in needlework. They created beautiful and functional clothing that kept their families warm and dry in the arctic weather.

Knitting first came to Alaska in the hands of missionaries. It was a hidden gift that arrived in a cultural collision.

Early Russian and European visitors to Alaska found the conditions under which the Native Alaskans were living appalling, because their lifestyle was so different from

European expectations. In addition to making trade agreements with the indigenous peoples to collect furs, the newcomers felt an obligation to "civilize" the established residents. They introduced them to modern conveniences, such as whiskey and iron. They also converted them to Christianity. They set up churches and schools in the area and worked hard to convince the Native people to abandon many of their centuries-old traditions. The missionaries persuaded the men to abandon the men's houses, completely changing the family structure and the organization of culture and daily life. When the men moved from the community houses into their family houses, the women were no longer autonomous. Although churches, schools, and trading posts sometimes substituted for community gathering places, they did not provide the links to the past lifestyle that had served these people effectively for thousands of years. Missionaries also introduced foreign foods such as flour, raisins, and other packaged foods, which were available year-round for cash. These new trade goods required a different sort of economy, and they edged out what had been a healthy, seasonal diet of foods acquired from and appropriate to the environment. The Native way of life was changing, and it was not an easy transition.

Along with their religion and customs, missionaries brought yarn and knitting needles. They put these new tools into the hands of the first Alaskan knitters. What those knitters did with these tools became one of the ways they were able to maintain their independence, while operating within the different cultural dynamics that had been brought without invitation into their world.

I learned to knit from a Russian, too—my grandmother. For as long as I can remember, my grandmother always had several projects on the needles. Old black and white photos in my family albums show the sweaters she made for herself and for my mother and uncle before I was born. My grandmother loved to knit, and to give the finished projects to her children and grandchildren. For as long as I can remember, my grandmother also had a job. My grandfather had been in poor health for many years and had to retire early. Grandma worked on the side to make some extra money to keep the refrigerator filled. Although she was a hard worker and never complained, she would never have dreamed of knitting for money, for economic imperative.

Once the missionaries introduced knitting to Alaska, it became a popular craft. Just as in the lower 48, knitting in Alaska started out as a necessary tool for making clothing and it later became a hobby. Although knitting allowed women to make garments for less money than they cost in the store, it was not initially recognized as a way to *make* money, to generate income, and to bring into people's lives the power to make choices about how and where they would live.

In the 1950s, a Vermonter named John Teal had a vision to domesticate an animal native to Alaska and to create a cottage industry that would provide income to Native Alaskan people living in villages across the state. Teal was concerned about poverty and education; he believed that musk-ox domestication could be a tool for bringing financial security to rural communities in Alaska. With the coming of the cash economy and modern technology to

Eskimo villages, Teal foresaw that new sources of income would be necessary. While he assumed "the minority must become acculturated," he believed that "social responsibility is recognized, to reduce the cultural chaos inevitably resulting from transition." After running an experimental farm for ten years in Vermont, Teal started a full-sized domestication project working with musk oxen in Alaska. He began shaping a plan to develop yarn and products that Alaskan residents could sell to tourists. By the late 1960s, the farm was considered a success, qiviut yarn was being processed from the animals' soft underdown fiber, and it was time to start knitting.

In 1968, nine women attended the first workshop meetings over the Christmas holidays in Mekoryuk on Nunivak Island. In the following months, another twenty-one knitters completed the lessons and made qiviut scarves. As other villages became interested, it was soon obvious that the project was going to be a success. In 1970, Oomingmak Musk Ox Producers' Co-operative was incorporated. Knitting was becoming a way to help keep the refrigerator full and give women economic power that could sustain their families and allow them to continue significant portions of their traditional ways of life.

All of this I learned from books and magazines, as my passion to learn about the Oomingmak knitters led me to the library and onto the Internet. At the time, I was working as a technical writer and creating computer manuals for high-tech corporations. After changing jobs four times in almost as many years, I finally realized that it wasn't just the job I hated, it was the entire industry. I decided I would rather surround myself with yarn and knitters than computers and engineers. While I was reading about Oomingmak and the Native Alaskan culture, I sent some of my designs to magazines. Amazingly, the editors liked my work and asked for more. I decided to try my hand at a bigger project and wrote a book of knitting patterns. The first printing sold out in a few months. I began to think I was onto something. Perhaps my obsession with qiviut and Alaska could be turned into another book. In 2004, I decided to visit Alaska to learn about the co-op and meet the knitters in person.

The Oomingmak co-op's headquarters and retail shop are housed in a small building at the corner of 6th and H streets in downtown Anchorage. The co-operative is named after the musk ox, known as the "bearded one," *oomingmak,* in the Inupiat language. The knitters of Oomingmak use yarn spun from musk ox down to make elegant knitted lace and warm color-patterned accessories in natural hues. Airy images of harpoons, Yup'ik dancers, and butterflies inspired by ancient artifacts adorn hand-knit scarves, nachaq hoods, and caps. Fluffy patterns of snowflakes and musk oxen adorn the colorwork hats and headbands. The shop in downtown Anchorage is the centralized action point for this enterprise. It sells these luxury items to tourists and handles all of the business paperwork and logistics, but the Oomingmak co-op extends throughout Alaska, with much of its work taking place in knitters' homes in the scattered, often geographically isolated, villages.

Each member of Oomingmak pays a $2 annual membership fee. Members do not pay for yarn; their working materials are provided by the co-op. They do have to purchase their own knitting needles. Knitters correspond with the co-op primarily by mail. Because few of the knitters live near or in Anchorage, and travel in Alaska is quite expensive, the knitters receive their yarn by mail, send back finished items by the same means, and then watch the post for more yarn, which comes along with their payment.

The knitters are paid by the stitch, and they are paid when their items are completed, not when the final retail sale is made. Each project has a specific number of stitches cast on and a specific number of rows to knit, so the total can easily be calculated. The actual price per stitch changes over time, so it has kept pace with inflation, but the goal is to give the knitters fair compensation for their work while keeping the prices of the finished items at a level that will not make them seem unreasonable to tourists. At the end of the year, any profit is distributed to the knitters, each of whom receives a percentage based on the number of items she knit during the year.

Because the knitters of the co-op are doing production knitting, some members get tired of knitting the same thing over and over again. (Many hobbyist knitters can relate, knowing how difficult it can be to finish the second in a pair of socks or mittens!) However, there is some variety built into the available choices. Several different items can be knit by each member in the signature pattern of her village, including scarves, stoles, and nachaq hoods. There are also several lace hats with designs that can be made by knitters in any village. The colorwork knitters can knit any of the patterns in the Tundra and Snow collection, which includes four different headbands and six different hats. However, the co-op members knit primarily to make money, not for pleasure. Once they become proficient in knitting a specific pattern, they can knit much faster and more accurately by specializing.

While I was in Alaska, I met with Fran Degnan, one of the Oomingmak knitters who lives in the village of Unalakleet. Fran is an inspiring and fascinating woman who is passionate about preserving the environment for future generations, through the wise use of both renewable and non-renewable resources. She lives the traditional Eskimo subsistence lifestyle and also has the versatility to move into the mainstream American culture when necessary to stand up for Native Alaskan rights. Meeting her was the highlight of my trip to Unalakleet. As I was reading Fran's book, Under the Arctic Sun*, I realized that bit-by-bit, one small decision after another, the Yup'ik and Inupiat have been slowly and voluntarily assimilating the Outsiders' ways. I guess in part it is necessary to do this in order to have a political voice in the dominant governmental system, to have their voices heard on state and federal decision-making committees. In part, the convenience of new technologies is irresistible: electricity, running water, and snowmobiles make some parts of life much easier. Some technologies and new customs have been adopted to improve health. But even though Fran and others mention the health benefits on the one hand (clean water and sewer systems, access to modern medical facilities), they prefer the old, natural ways of tradition on the other (not taking drugs, eating fresh and local foods).*

Unalakleet is a medium-sized village of about 600 people on the west coast of Alaska. It has a post office, a school, two state troopers, and a general store. Most of the other jobs available are in commercial fishing, which is seasonal work. In a place where high-paying jobs are few and far between, the costs of basic necessities are outrageously high. A pack of hot dogs costs $7, a gallon of milk is $6.99, a quart of apple juice is $4.59, and one pound of low-quality chop meat costs $3.49. In addition, most of the food filling the shelves of the general store is processed and frozen. The selection of fresh, healthy items is all but non-existent. This is true all over the Yukon-Kuskokwim River Delta, where most of the knitters from the Oomingmak co-op live. With so few opportunities to make money and little healthy food available for sale even at high prices, the people still depend primarily on traditional food-gathering techniques for their survival.

Most of the Yup'ik people who live in the delta work hard to preserve their Native traditions and live off the land, but that does not eliminate the need for cash. Today, snowmobiles have largely replaced dog teams for winter transportation, and aluminum fishing boats have replaced kayaks for summer travel. Both types of vehicles run on purchased fuel. Traditional fur parkas have been replaced by modern polar fleece and ready-to-wear winter clothing. Indoor plumbing, heated houses, and computers have become necessities of life in Eskimo villages, just as they have elsewhere. These are just a few examples of how modern technologies are being incorporated into the traditional subsistence lifestyle. And all of these things cost money.

Traditional Yup'ik society was much more egalitarian than today's free-market culture. Wealth was often redistributed at annual feasts and ceremonies, and families took care of one another in a way that is not common in modern American society. The changes that have come, in many places just over the past forty or fifty years, have not been easy for many Yup'ik and Inupiat people to accept. They struggle to maintain the important aspects of their culture, while adopting modern tools to help them gain a stronger political voice and to make life easier for themselves and their children.

Knitting gives women in these villages the ability to make money while they travel to fish camps and berry-picking areas in the summer, preserve food for the coming winter each fall, and care for young children or elders throughout the year.

I had a lot to think about after my trip to Alaska. I wanted to stay longer, but after two weeks of traveling around the state with my husband, who was taking pictures, I ran out of money. When I came home, I started writing my book while I was still working on writing computer manuals. Somewhere between the end of my trip and finishing the manuscript, the excitement about what I was doing got lost in the stress of working two jobs at once. When the deadline for my book came, I was not finished. I had never missed a work deadline before, and I started to worry about what was wrong with me. I went to see my doctor, and she said that extreme procrastination could be a sign of depression. Fortunately, recognizing that I had a problem seemed to be my cure and I did not need to take any

drugs or go to a therapist. I decided to stop working on com-
puter jobs, even if it meant I would make less than half of
the money I'd been used to. If knitting could give me a way to
make money with less stress, I was going to try it.

Although all of the knitters in the Oomingmak co-op are
Native Alaskan women, they are a diverse group. Some
grew up in sod houses, others never saw the traditional
dwellings as children. Some still go to fish camp every
spring, pick berries, and eat local foods almost exclusively.
Others have never participated in subsistence activities, or
have done so only as children. Today, just as in the lower
48, many women learn to knit from their mothers, grandmothers, aunts, and neighbors, and continue to make
clothing for themselves and gifts for friends and family
members. Other knitters learned to knit in workshops presented by Oomingmak, and only knit for extra income.
Some knitters remain in their home villages and others have
moved to Anchorage for jobs or to attend college. Teens,
young mothers, college students, senior citizens, and village
elders knit for Oomingmak. They bring in between $15
and $5,000 a year through knitting. They often provide a
substantial supplement to their family's income that allows
them to choose how they will live.

Life for women in the Alaskan bush is still more difficult than it is for those of us who live in cities, suburbs, and
even in rural towns in the lower 48. The knitters of
Oomingmak live in small villages scattered across the vast,
open spaces of Alaska. Each village has a unique history
and a distinctive culture that blends traditional Yup'ik and

Inupiat subsistence activities with modern jobs at local airports, general stores, and public schools. Unemployment is high in most Native Alaskan villages, with seasonal work available on fishing boats and in construction. Many of these jobs are filled by men. Knitting provides one way for the women to have economic freedom.

At the beginning of the twenty-first century, the villages along the Bering Sea continue a journey from past to future, merging traditional and modern culture at their own pace, as local elders and community leaders make decisions and instigate changes they feel are best for their people. The knitters of Oomingmak are capturing traditional designs in a modern craft, while providing themselves a way to make money and still participate in their unique and time-honored culture. Their work preserves their cultural heritage, and they take pride in the high quality of their fine needlework. As their needles click across Alaska, in cities and rural villages, in living rooms and kitchens, at fish camps and even in boats, the knitters of Oomingmak are answering the call of economic imperative and self determination.

Here at my home in Colorado, knitting gives me a way to escape the drudgery of everyday work and to explore the world, even when I can't get on a plane and fly to the Alaskan bush. This year, for the first time, I did not have to take on any computer jobs for money. I no longer spend my days doing work I hate, commuting in traffic to sit all day in a cubicle, and putting in long hours to fill the pocket of a rich CEO. I no longer dream of changing my life. Today I am at peace with myself and my work, and I spend my time writing about things

I love, things that may help to bring more peace and under-standing to the world. Today, I also knit to answer the call of economic imperative and self determination.

Butterfly pattern by Donna Druchunas
Reproduced by permission from Donna Druchunas, Arctic Lace: Knitting Projects and Stories Inspired by Alaska's Native Knitters *(Fort Collins, CO: Nomad Press, 2006), page 165.*

Snohomish couple in temporary summer house, Puget Sound, Washington, 1905. Norman Edson.

I love, things that may help to bring more peace and under-standing to the world. Today, I also knit to answer the call of economic imperative and self determination.

Butterfly Pattern
Note: Only RS rows are shown, purl WS rows.

Because the zigzag lines on this pattern are continuous with no plain knit sts between repeats, you must read the chart differently for flat and circular knitting.

For flat knitting:
± Work as ⟋, except in last repeat, then work as ⟍.
Work st 1 at beg of row, then repeat shaded sts for desired number of repeats, end with last st at end of row.

For circular knitting:
± Work as ⟋.
Do *not* work first and last sts of chart

Butterfly pattern by Donna Druchunas
Reproduced by permission from Donna Druchunas, Arctic Lace: Knitting Projects and Stories Inspired by Alaska's Native Knitters *(Fort Collins, CO: Nomad Press, 2006), page 165.*

Snohomish couple in temporary summer house, Puget Sound, Washington, 1905. Norman Edson.

Photos of, and references to, Native Americans knitting date back to the mid-nineteenth century, and include both men and women from a variety of tribes: Tigua and Pueblo (New Mexico), Snohomish, Nooksack and Skagit (Washington State), Mohegan (Connecticut), Nez Perce (Idaho), and Hopi (Arizona). Though not a craft traditional to any tribe, some Native Americans incorporated ancestral basketweaving and other designs into their knitting. Many learned to knit from white settlers and missionaries. In the Southwest, they learned from the Spanish, according to Kathy Whitaker, Director of the Indian Arts Research Foundation in New Mexico, who adds that it was Hopi men, rather than women, who knit because it was they who used the finished knitted garments for ceremonial dances. Steve Grafe of the National Cowboy Museum offers the following citations regarding Nez Perce knitting, under the auspices of Eliza Henry Spalding, who served with her husband as a Presbyterian missionary at the Clearwater Mission

Photo opposite: Man and woman sit in their beach hut, by fire, under fish smoking rack. She is knitting, with yarn in woven basket. (Note from unidentified source): Snohomish Indians on Puget Sound, during the summer in 1905—before and after—erected temporary dwellings on the shore composed of rush mats and pieces of canvas, and hung their salmon catch on beams above a camp fire to be smoked and cured for the winter months.

Credit: University of Washington Libraries, Special Collections, NA710

Station (present-day Spalding, Ohio) from 1836–1847:
Mrs. S[p]alding has regularly about her a number of young females, which she is teaching to Card, Spin, Weave Blankets & Knit stockings. Mr. S[palding] has a great many hand Looms, & he showed me blankets which have been wove[n] by a Native on one of these which was not much inferior to Mackinaws. [1]

Grafe notes that Eliza Spalding, writing to her sister shortly thereafter, also commented on the activity:

With my assistance the women have made 24 yards of good substantial woolen cloth... They look to me much more comfortable and respectable in these dresses than in any others I have ever seen them wear. They have also knit for themselves yellow stockings... [and three] have knit themselves leggings...

Some appearance of civilization and improvement I think, we now really see. [2]

As with the Oomingmak cooperative knitters today [see preceding essay, "Knitting Softens the Impact as Worlds Collide" by Donna Druchunas, beginning on pg. 128], Native Americans in times past used knitting as a means to raise much-needed cash. A Nooksack named Louisa George was born in 1894, and her life history was documented by the Center for Pacific Northwest Studies at Western Washington University. She picked berries; worked in a cannery; and knit socks, sweaters, and afghans to sell in order to eke out a living. Faith Damon Davison, archivist of the Mohegan Tribe, remarks that handwork was sold in the mid-nineteenth century at church festivals in order to pay for coal and other necessities.

[1] *1841 from O.B. Sperlin, ed., "Our First Horticulturist—The Brackenridge Journal," Part 3,* Washington Historical Quarterly *22.1 (1931): 51–52)*

[2] *Clifford M. Drury,* First White Women Over the Rockies: Diaries, Letter, and Biographical Sketches of Six Women of the Oregon Mission Who Made the Overland Journey in 1836 and 1838, *Vol. 1: Mrs. Marcus Whitman, Mrs. Henry H. Spalding, Mrs. William H. Gray, and Mrs. Asa B. Smith (Glendale, CA: Arthur H. Clark, 1963) 215*

Excerpts from an interview with
Mrs. Elizabeth E. Miller

West Newbury, Vermont
by Mrs. Rebecca M. Halley
November 18, 1938

Grammy Miller is not very tall, but she is heavy. Her body is square and solid. Her hair is gray and sweeps up to a loose knot on top of her head. She wears a gingham dress, an apron, and when she stops to sit down she draws a square of shawl over her broad shoulders. Her face is wide and strong; her eyes are intent and interested. She peers at one in concentration, for her sight is clouded by cataracts which, she says, will make her blind, if (she adds quaintly) she lives long enough. Vigorous hairs spring out on her chin and round her mouth. Her wrinkles are deep with hard, intense living. Laugh wrinkles, anger wrinkles, scorn wrinkles, worry wrinkles. Her face is a map of her life. She has a deep, booming, easy laugh. She likes strong talk, strong living, strong people.

There is no weakness in her and she cannot abide it in others. She carries and flaunts a deep and consuming pride in her own, both sons and grandchildren. They were afraid of her in the days when she was the patriarch of the family. New ways and customs have weakened her power. She is still vitally interested in all the world is doing and would rather discuss present events and trends than those of the past. Her creed has been and is, "work hard, work well, save something out of everything you earn." She has been a hard, merciless woman, but time and sorrow have mellowed her to rich understanding woven through with a gleaming vein of humor. Her feet have given out and she finds it hard to get around. "I will not give up," she says, "for if I should take to my bed, I would never be out of it. I would rather wear out than rust out... "

"I was the oldest of six children. Mother was never very well and when I was about ten she was taken real sick and had to be abed most of the time. We had help sometimes, but as soon as I could, I took over and did the work...

"Father had a loom; it was grandmother's. It was broken and I was always at him to get it fixed, but he never did. I felt bad about that for I wanted to learn to weave. I would spin for I learned to do that. We would take the sheep's wool to the mill and have it carded into rolls. Then I spun it. We had the spinning wheel here until the old house burned down in 1926. So many things went then that meant so much to me. But I never let myself think about it. There's no use and it was hard enough for the boys without my complaining. About the spinning—I spun the warp, but mother thought she had better spin the filling. Bert Tuttle's grandmother was to weave the cloth and she came to the house to see the spinning. She looked at the warp and said to mother. 'My sakes, you better let this girl spin 'he filling, too. She has done a nice piece of work here.' Later she told mother she couldn't have had nicer, stronger yarn to weave with. She made up the cloth for a frock for father. It was a long frock that came clear to his knees made from wool of our own sheep.

"Mother and I knit all the long stockings for the women and girls and the footins and mittens from yarn I had spun. Land sakes, the footins, double mittens, and single mittens I have knit. After I was married and the children were growing up, I was never without a pair of needles in my hands. In the fall, I had somebody came in to help while I did up the fall spinning.

"Land sakes, don't you know how they spin? With my right hand or with a stick, some women used a stick, but I most usually used my hand, I would keep the wheel going and with my left I pulled the yarn and twisted it to the spindle." She demonstrated with both bands, the motions. "Then I had a swift to wind the yarn on. It was a whirly thing that let the yarn free to wind into a ball.

"Land sakes, one time I had company and they wanted to know how many skeins I had spun that day. I sent little Clarence in to get all the skeins. He was just a small young one then and he was loaded with the ten skeins. Granny

Miller lived with us then and she thought Clarence was the only child ever was. She would say, 'Aye, yon bairn war unca guide wee 'un.' She would call him 'Ma bonnie prince, ma wee king' and was in a fair way to spoil him.

"I always colored my own yarns and I would make the boys' stockings striped grey and some other pretty color like blue to go with it. The legs were knit with a row of color and the feet plain. When I went out to a sociable or a farmers' meeting in the evening, I always took my knitting. We had a spanking pair then and when we were out in the carryall I knit up hill and down. My knitting went everywhere but to church."

Credit: Library of Congress, Manuscript Division, WPA Federal Writers' Project Collection

Knitting Through...
Industrial Development

Knitting: My Urban Escape
by Barbara DeMarco Barrett

I am obsessed with knitting for some of the same reasons as other knitters: I love yarn and color; I love the repetitive motion of knitting; I love the singular items you can create. But recently, I had an epiphany about why I knit: Knitting is my reaction to living in the most industrialized country in the world.

I live in one of the wealthiest beach communities on the Southern California coast (how I got here is a whole other story), in a county—Orange County—that's more focused on the accumulation of wealth than on the things that matter—to me, anyway: originality, creativity, community.

This no doubt will seem wacky to a non-knitter, but I see knitters as people who've taken it on themselves to make life more beautiful. No knitter I know of sets out with the goal of making an ugly hat, sweater, or iPod cozy. But around the O.C., interior designers are the ones who do the beautifying, not the homeowners. (Do any of them even knit? More on that later.) Here at the southeastern edge of Newport Beach, residents covet granite kitchen counters, weekly manicures, designer purses, and glitzy cars. SUVs, Range Rovers and Mercedes—and, more and more (ergh!),

Hummers—crowd our skinny streets. Which is when that old Peggy Lee song, "Is That All There Is?" begins to play in my brain. It can't be enough, can it? I mean, seriously: Without knitting, what could ever be enough?

Of course, I exaggerate. And of course there are good, benevolent souls about who contribute good—even great—things to the area, who also worry over the frenzied pace of life, growing congestion and density, and materialism of this once tiny, placid town. Yet, they seem to be able to shrug it off. Those who can't, move. Me, I turn my worries to knitting. It's my medication *sans* side effects. It's one of the main ways I connect to how this town, and maybe even the world, used to be.

Corona del Mar is a dot on the coast between Los Angeles and San Diego. In the early part of the twentieth century, it was a weekend getaway for Los Angeles and Pasadena denizens who still had money after the Great Depression took so much from so many. The town remained a haven until the 1940s and 1950s, when developers began building bungalows for the weekenders. The surrounding land was farming country, given to agriculture and cattle.

Now Corona del Mar is one of the most densely populated towns around. Its coastal hillsides, which once sprouted mustard and chaparral, have been transformed into sculpted yards; multi-million dollar homes are squeezed into high-end subdivisions. (If I had a million dollars for a home, you can bet I'd seek out some real land and a sheep or two, not a cookie-cutter house shoved up against another expensive house, but maybe that's just me...)

Today, Corona del Mar is so unlike the Pennsylvania countryside where I lived for my first eleven years, where homes were surrounded by vast lawns and tall trees; on the way to school, I passed cows lingering in fields. This town is so at odds with the rural Vermont village where I lived while I was a college student. For most of those four years, a creek or waterfall flowed through my backyard; in one case, a waterfall *was* my backyard. It may have been like that in Corona del Mar when people first arrived, but formidable yards, meadows, and certainly creeks—if they even exist—are now the province of millionaires.

Cottages similar to the two-bedroom house that my husband, son, two cats, six fish, five storage bins–worth of yarn, and I inhabit will sell for at least a million dollars, often to developers who tear them down, eradicating history and handicraft. Earthmovers plow the ground as flat as an afghan, though not nearly so resplendent or quirky as a knitted one. Soon afterward, new construction ensues. Before long, a behemoth—of late, the rage is a faux-Italian villa—has gobbled up the entire lot and left no room for even a patch of green.

Yet, like so many self-employed creative folk, we continue to rent rather than buy an affordable condo (the cost of a home in this area or areas we like are out of range). One reason is that the schools are good here, but also there are few better sights than the magenta bougainvillea and purple morning glories climbing up and over the roof of our vintage house. Our home has character by the boatload.

Knitters—and artists of all kinds—are sensitive to their physical environments. We want them to be pleasing to us.

The thought of living in a condominium, squished between two other families, with cardboard walls and a view of garages, fills me with a sense of foreboding. To distract myself, I keep busy. Too busy, really. I write, teach, host a weekly radio show, volunteer, and knit. Oh, how I knit. Knitting helps me to exist as a stranger in a strange beach town—even stranger now that we no longer have the surf bums that Southern California celebrated in the 1950s and 1960s because they have been priced out of the neighborhood.

It's growing stranger all the time. Several weeks ago, at the end of the school day, I pulled into the parking lot of my son's middle school and found a space close to the entrance so he would see me when school let out. I buzzed the windows down. The sun blazed in a cloudless blue sky. Nearby, a pretty teenage girl shouted into her pink Razr phone, "Where the hell are you, Mom?" and I thought, Where am *I*, that kids curse at their parents on cell phones and their parents take it?

Cars lined up—mostly SUVs—with bored-looking women sitting motionless behind their steering wheels, many pressing cell phones against the sides of their faces, with the windows sealed shut. The lyrics from that old Animals song, another on the soundtrack of my life: "We gotta get outa this place, if it's the last thing we ever do..." pinged about my brain.

A sudden urge to knit came over me, as if at that moment, knitting was my lifeline to sanity. I eyed the green tote sitting on the passenger's seat. It held the beginnings of a bolero sweater I was knitting in a buttery soft, seafoam-shaded cotton blend. As I pulled out the project, I thought, "Y'all can freak out and be mean to your mothers, or sit in your new cars and shut out the world. I'm going to knit."

To think that our culture has become so insular was upsetting, but I felt rebellious—and lucky: I had something I loved doing, something that kept me from sitting there bored, motionless, looking spoiled and detached. It was at that very moment it occurred to me that knitting is one way I defy so much about what Orange County—and Southern California—now seems to represent. It is my way of saying, "No, I will not be consumed by all things commercial and manufactured." I could buy handmade sweaters, shawls, and purses. Yet, spending hundreds on a handmade blanket or sweater seems decadent and wasteful, while constructing them with my own hands and heart strikes me as nurturing and a contribution to the greater good, somehow.

Here in the O.C., when women—and girls, even—admire my knitting, they ask how much I'd sell it for. This astounds me, perhaps more than it should. For instance, my felted intarsia getaway satchel couldn't go for less than two grand, given the gobs of painstaking time it took, I tell them. At first, they think I'm kidding; then they admit that of course, it *should* sell for that much. Mostly, no matter what they ask about, I say, "It's not for sale, but I'll teach you." Inevitably, they laugh nervously and proceed to tell me why they could never learn. I tell them knitting directions were once hard for me, too, but that doesn't sway them. Often they change the subject—because they don't have the confidence to knit, or because they couldn't be bothered with such a plebian pastime?

Are they not experiencing what I am? In this overdeveloped corner of the world, where orange groves and bean fields have been plowed under to make room for more and more new homes, I need to stay as connected as I can. Knitting is a way to do this. I want to tell these women: Everything we create—pies, paintings, songs—resonates with our deepest needs as human beings, as *creative* beings, to make things of beauty and worth. It's this act of creation that allows our souls to breathe, enables us to activate our spiritual selves and connect with nature. How could they be missing this?

My friend Deborah, whom I met on an online forum, says, "Knitting is a productive diversion: You get something out of it and it is also an artistic expression, which does a lot for personal pride. For those of us who are more tactile and like to feel and see things, it does something with that too, but I don't know how to formally express this. I adore knitting face cloths and there is something very therapeutic about them when used with water."

My father was a shoe designer. He came from Sicily when he was a teen, entered the country via Ellis Island, and years later was designing shoes in New York, then in Pennsylvania. (An early iteration of the saddle shoe was his.) My mother's dad left Naples for Pennsylvania, where he worked as a train crossing guard. During downtime, he made folk art—wooden dioramas of crucifixion scenes—in bottles. The last twenty years of her life, my mother crocheted—mostly afghans that threatened to swallow her whole, the larger they grew. Handiwork runs in my veins, or perhaps we all share the same nervous streak on which creativity grows like yeast on sugar.

Handling yarn, working with color and texture, and passing it through my fingers stitch by stitch until it is transformed into something beautiful or fun soothes *and* excites me, all at once. It also affects my mood. As I knit my son Travis a log cabin blanket from *Mason Dixon Knitting*, which builds from the center using strips of color, I remember a not-so-known book by Dr. Seuss, *My Many Colored Days*, which I read to Travis when he was small.

When I'm knitting with purple, I feel a bit royal, somewhat heady. Pink, and my mood lifts; how can you not feel even a little happy when you're knitting with pink? Red, I feel a tad passionate and fired up. I love using shades of soothing blues; they relax me when I'm in need of slowing down. Gray—no thanks. I'm already depressed enough. The colors that we knitters use affect our psyches, whether we like it or not, and that is half the enjoyment of knitting.

Knitting is one of the most pleasurable ways I know to create things that others can enjoy over the long term. I may be in the minority here, but I'd rather receive a gift someone made for me, however flawed, than something bought, which is *so* not Orange County. I like that Brian wears socks I made just for him. He calls the first pair of socks his "$1,000 socks" because, had I used that time working rather than knitting, I would have earned as much. I like that the felted intarsia guitar strap I designed and knit for him hugs his slim frame when he's onstage. When I'm working on the log cabin blanket for my son and people ask what I'm making, Travis chimes in, "She's making a blanket for *me*." I love that he's proud that I would use my time and skill to make something for him, and I'm gratified to know he appreciates the value of one-of-a-kind handmade items. When we create original things, we exert control over an aspect of our lives; it's so necessary when life seems so *out* of control and so all over the place.

When it comes right down to it, knitting is my way of expressing hope and love—and it's one of the prime ways I stay sane. I marvel at the power that two sticks and a ball of yarn can wield over millions of women—and men—and how knitting keeps all of us centered.

Despite the attitude of my fellow O.C. residents, I knew I couldn't be alone in my attraction to knitting as a way to deal with living in a less-than-ideal environment. I wanted to hear other knitters' thoughts on the topic, so I went searching for like-minded souls.

Maribeth, another forum friend from Virginia, says, "Knitting and spinning [do] so much for me in this zoo they call progress. It keeps me grounded, calm, cloaked with independence (self-sufficient and different than the herd), creative, and imaginative (hard to do in a town of clones), in touch with nature, and helps me keep my sense of humor. And for those who laugh over my knitting and give me the 'Oh, you are *so* domestic,' with raised eyebrows, they get a mental raspberry blown at them. . . . I love knitting because it helps blind me to the waste and materialistic area where I live."

I hardly understand it myself—this ability knitting has to absorb your thoughts and feelings and turn them into a more positive, benevolent direction. But whoever heard of an angry knitter? Knitting's tactile, earthy quality and its link to a simpler way of life draws me to it, and I welcome such a diversion.

"Part of why I like to knit," says Susan from California, "is that I've always longed to have a more down-to-earth life. I would love to live in the wide-open spaces with a garden and some chickens and even some sheep. Instead, I live in a somewhat run-down apartment in the suburbs." She says that knitting—and cooking—helps her to live her life, as much as possible, "as though I lived in the country."

When I asked Nova Scotia–based knitter/designer/world traveler Jane Thornley for her thoughts about knitting as a means of coping with urban sprawl, thinking, *she's already in the country, in Nova Scotia. No urban sprawl there, nor stress.* She said, "Knitting is a means to cope, period. Besides being a metaphor for connectivity, the soothing rhythm coupled with the creativity makes it a perfect antidote for everything life throws in one's path. In urban California, with its speed, the concrete highways (reminding me of hardening of the arteries) and increasing crime, knitting represents all that we see as human in a frantic existence. I can only say that it must be a challenge to live an authentic life in your beautiful state. On one hand, here's a state populated by some of the most creative and dynamic of humans and yet everyone's crammed together with a frequently surreal aesthetic: a preoccupation with outward appearance compounded by a split-second philosophy-to-go lifestyle."

You're telling me!

Last week I did battle on those concrete highways Jane Thornley mentioned, to visit a yarn store not far from my house to pick up a few random things: size 1 double pointed bamboo needles to make finger puppets for a friend's baby, a skein of blood-red cotton yarn for Travis' log cabin blanket-in-progress, and a skein of chartreuse Rowan Cashmerino for a pair of fingerless gloves I've been yearning to knit to try my hand at cables. Lisa, one of the owners, delicately packaged the items in a brown paper bag with a handle and pushed a sheet of olive green tissue paper down into it, which made my purchase feel more like a gift than supplies.

Back in the car, I put the bag on the floor near the console. Every so often, stopped at a red light, I picked up the bag and peered inside, pulled out a skein of yarn or the needles, and smiled.

For now, I accept that I live in a region that's increasingly hard to relate to, where freeway traffic jams, bad air, and the stress of pending earthquakes rattle each day and invade the simple acts of driving and living. Yet, in the cocoon of my minivan, at that moment, as I listened to a book on CD and stole glances at my new knitting supplies beside me, I was fine. For a time, anyway, I was giddy with expectation. I would soon be home, away from the fray, and back at the needles.

EXCERPT FROM "AN UNFINISHED STOCKING,
NEW ENGLAND, 1837"

Depending on one's perspective, an unfinished stocking shows work in motion or work arrested. That round balls of unbleached linen remained attached to a stocking that was never finished suggests that its value lay outside the thread. No one knows who began it or why it was saved. It might represent a life interrupted by death or some long forgotten woman's feckless vow to get back to her knitting when she could. Perhaps it was lost in the bottom of a trunk or basket and emerging at a time when factory production had transformed it into a curiosity. Whatever its origins, it looks back to the colonial period and forward to the age of domesticity by knitting together the complex strands of female life.

Although imported stockings, many of them made on an ingenious machine called a "knitting frame," were available from the seventeenth century on, hand-knitting was ubiquitous throughout the colonial period and into the early republic. Mary Rowlandson unraveled and knitted stockings for her captors in a Nipmuck village in 1676. In 1769, seven "Ladies of the first Fashion" in Newport, Rhode Island, supported the cause of liberty by joining "in the laudable Business of KNITTING." On a Colchester, Connecticut, farmstead a few years later, Betty Foot worked at her knitting as "stiddy as a Priest." In coastal Maine, Eliza Wildes packed hand-spun and hand-knitted stockings into her husband's sea chest, while along the Kennebec, midwife Martha Ballard knitted stockings during lulls in her patients' labors.

Source: Ulrich, Laurel Thatcher. The Age of Homespun: Objects and Stories in the Creation of an American Myth. *New York: Vintage Books, 2002, pgs. 375–6.*

Knitting Through...
Families in Motion

Excerpts from "A Greek Mother"

Living Lore in New England, New Hampshire Federal Writers' Project by Evanthea Keriazes

From the sunny section of the southern European Balkan Countries, some twenty years ago, the lovely Basilike (Bessie) Zikou came to the United States. That dark-eyed girl is now my mother, Mrs. Andrew Keriazes, still young and vivacious, though she is the mother of nine children.

At night, as we sit around the living room fireplace in our six-room house, we ask our mother to tell us stories of her childhood days spent in Macedonia, Greece. Our fingers are busy cracking the rich brown chestnuts, but hers, never idle, are guiding the flying knitting needles in and out of the yards and yards of stout woolen yarn which are growing into innumerable scarves, mittens, and other winter [clothes] for the younger boys and girls... [W]e chatter and joke in the native Greek which is spoken in our household. But mother's stories are the highlights and we never tire of hearing them over and over again...

[W]e have learned from our mother's stories that during her childhood... she had little time for play. Although the village tailor made her boleros and full long skirts, she made all the skirts, trousers and various articles worn by the other members of the family... "Our winter nights were spent in knitting, embroidering, and weaving, for both the cloth and the blankets were made from the wool of our own sheep," she says. Then she adds, "We were not as fortunate about play as you children here in America. In summer I worked most of the time either in the garden or went with my youngest sister and Bashou, our faithful sheepdog, to tend the flock upon the mountain side, while my brothers helped our father in odd pieces of work like carrying stones to repair the walls or hoeing in the vineyards. We had a village school but we were not made to go. I could not be spared often, so I only attended it in winter, for in summer there was too much work to be done."

Credit: Library of Congress, Manuscript Division, WPA Federal Writers' Project Collection

A Greek peasant woman spinning yarn by hand, 1901. Unknown photographer.

Credit: Library of Congress, Prints & Photographs Division, reproduction #LC-USZ62-65924

Yarn homespun as in the above picture is, more often than not, extremely rough. Combined with the high tension created by the Greek method of knitting, the resulting fabric made by such craftswomen of old was "like iron," according to the book, *Knitting Around the World*. To knit in the Greek fashion, "[T]he yarn is tensioned behind the neck and looped onto the right needle with the left thumb, which holds it in front of the work. Since the yarn is in front, purling is much easier than knitting. To knit, the right needle must be pushed upward through the stitch in front of the left needle."

Knitting Through It

Excerpts from an Interview with J. L. Tarter

Folk Stuff—Life on a Range by Sheldon F. Gauthier

"So that one may know how we made our living, I shall explain what and how we did, which was typical of country then in that section of Kentucky...

"We raised and sold a few cattle, mules, hogs, sheep, chickens, geese, and geese feathers. We grew apples and sold a little of those both green and dried. Also, we raised and sold some wheat and oats.

"Mother and sisters knitted woolen socks and mittens, from yarn grown and spun by them, and sold hundreds of pairs.

"We lived on the supply of food produced on the farm and the clothes we wore was made from cloth that was spun and weaved from material produced on the farm.

"Father and the oldest boys trapped and hunted, and we made winter caps from the animals hides, also, coon and other skins were sold.

"Judging from what I have mentioned as sold by the family, one may think there was a large income, but the contrary is the fact. For instance, eggs sold for five and ten cents a dozen. A pair of hand knitted woolen socks sold for 25¢ and all other articles accordingly...

"Our Winter clothing was made from wool carded, spun and woven into cloth, by my mother and sisters. Our Summer clothes were made from flax, which was grown on the farm...

"The amusements, for the most part, was husking-bees, logrollings for the men and quilting for the women, and once a year regularly the revival meeting for all."

Credit: Library of Congress, Manuscript Division, WPA Federal Writers' Project Collection

Mrs. Mary E. Burleson — Pioneer Story

Carrizozo, New Mexico
by Edith L. Crawford
February 1938

"The Government train we came to New Mexico in had about one hundred prairie schooners in it. Of this number four belonged to my family. My grandfather and grandmother Searcy, with six girls and one boy and my father, O. K. Chittenden, with my mother brother Tom and myself. I was five years old and my brother was about one year old. My grandfather and my father sold their farms in West Fort, Missouri. We brought all our supplies along with us. We had our flour in barrels, our own meat, lard and sugar. We were not allowed to stop and hunt buffalo on the way out here on account of the Indians. The women made the bread out of sour dough and used Soda. There was no such thing as baking powder in those days. The men baked the bread in Dutch ovens over the campfires. When we stopped at night the schooners with families were put into a circle and the Government schooners would form a circle around the family wagons. In between the two circles they put the oxen and horses, to keep the Indians from getting to them. Every night the men took turns standing guard. All the soldiers rode horses. Every few days the train would stop and everybody would get rested. The feet of the oxen would get so sore that they could not go without resting them every few days. When the train stopped it was nearly always at water and the women would do their washing. The train used cow and buffalo chips and anything they could find to burn. The men did all this as the women and children were never allowed far from the schooners on account of Indians. We did not milk our cow as she had to be worked along with the oxen. Our schooners had cowhides fastened underneath and our cooking utensils were packed in them. Our drinking water was carried in barrels tied to the sides of the schooners...

We left the wagon train on Raton Pass... When we found our new home—hard dirt floors and a dirt roof—my mother was so very homesick to go back to Missouri where we had a nice farm home. My mother had brought her spinning wheel with her. She spun all the yarn for our clothes and knitted all our socks and stockings. My father and grandfather made a loom for her and she made us two carpets for our floors to keep the baby from getting so awful dirty on the floor. We had brought some seed cane with us and my father and grandfather made a homemade syrup mill and made syrup, the first ever made in that country. The mill was a crude affair made of logs and drawn by a horse. The juice was pressed out with the logs and put in a vat and cooked into syrup. People came from miles around to see this mill."

Credit: Library of Congress, Manuscript Division, WPA Federal Writers' Project Collection

EXCERPT FROM "THE BANKS OF THE OHIO," PUBLISHED BY L. DEMING, BOSTON, MASSACHUSETTS, CIRCA 1876

Come all you fair maidens wherever you may be,
Come join in with us, and rewarded you will be:
Girls, if you'll card, knit, and spin, we'll plow, reap, and sow,
And will settle on the banks of the pleasant Ohio;
Girls, if you'll card, knit, and spin, we'll plow, reap, and sow,
And we'll fold you in our arms while the stormy wind
    doth blow.

Credit: Library of Congress, Rare Books and Special Collections Division, America Singing: Nineteenth-Century Song Sheets.

Between the years 1886 and 1912, Nebraska photographer Solomon D. Butcher created more than 3,000 photographs chronicling pioneer life on the Great Plains. Among the areas he documented was Cherry County during the "open range days" of cowboys and cattle—a period that lasted until 1885, when a preponderance of new settlers claiming once-wild prairie forced ranches farther west. According to

Family on ranch in Cherry County Nebraska, c. 1901 by Solomon D. Butcher.
Credit: Nebraska State Historical Society Photograph Collections

the Library of Congress, "It was the photographer's intention to record the process of homesteading, which he shrewdly recognized as a transient, yet important, epoch in the story of the American West. Butcher's photographs are not confined strictly to the homesteading experience. They document the construction of a new way of life; a new way of living never before attempted."

Knitting Through...
Relationships

Him & Her

EXCERPTS FROM AN INTERVIEW WITH
CARRIE SAIN (FARM WIFE)

NEWTON, NORTH CAROLINA
BY ETHEL DEAL
OCTOBER 10, 1939

Inside the little store, whose crude signs on the windows announced, "Groceries, Meats and Produce," Carrie Sain looked up from her knitting, pushed a bag of peanuts from the other end of the orange crate on which she was sitting, and asked me to have a seat.

"Yes, Bob Sain expects me to keep house and stay in the store too. It's a good thing I was raised on a farm, in a family of fifteen children, and learned how to work. I did manage to finish high school and go one year to college; I wanted to be a teacher. I taught nine years before marriage and six since.

"Bob bought a farm before we were married and I taught to help pay for it. He is one of the best farmers in the country, but the trouble with him was he drunk enough since we been married to buy three or four farms. What he didn't drink up he wasted and run through with. My children are all out on their own now, but his drinking made it hard on them when they were growing up...

"About four years ago he got so bad I sent him to the State Hospital for the Criminal Insane, but he stayed only four weeks. The doctors told him if he drank any more it would kill him. He craved the stuff so he suffered terribly, and took it out on us. He ran all the children away from home. After holding out eight months he started again. He gets on a drunk once in a while now and it nearly kills him...

"Bob's health is so bad now he can't do much work on the farm, so I have to look after it. We opened this business here a few years ago. He makes trips to the mountains and buys produce and cattle, while I look after the store and the farm. We keep a man hired on the farm and with my management we raise a lot of truck we can sell here in the store. I handle milk, butter and cheese from eight cows and show a nice profit. Bob has a wood saw, buys his wood in large quantities and sells it by the load when it's sawed. That shows a profit too.

"Back when Bob was drinking so much things on the farm run down something awful. He wouldn't spend a cent on the inside nor out. I thought we had reached the bottom when the house caught fire and burned down. We lived in the well house and grainary for two years before we could build again. The girls now are doing things. I have a nice seven room house painted inside and out. The girls have bought new rugs and furniture. The lawn is no longer a place to turn the cows. For the first time in my life I'm not ashamed to have company. Bob is still mean and takes out his drinking on me. I stay in the store and when business is dull I knit and read... Good times wasn't made for me. I've worked so long and played so little I've got out of the habit.

"I feel old. My skin goes uncared for. I never have time to have my hair done; Bob would think it was a waste of money if I did. I get up every morning and milk eight cows, while my youngest girl cooks breakfast. The milk must be strained and put away, and churning done. I'm usually at the store at nine o'clock. I've got no time to sew and do things to my clothes. I hire my laundry so to have more time to help Bob. I used to read a lot at night; now I'm so tired, I just go to bed..."

Carrie's work worn hands flew back and forth with the needles. Her nails were broken and ugly. The lines in her face told of hard work and sleepless nights. Her dark hair streaked with grey and cut in a boyish bob was oily and unkept. The dark grey flannel dress was made with no attempt as to fit or style and seemed ready to burst under the pressure of her hundred and eighty pounds of flesh. Numerous runs in her cheap rayon stockings accentuated the thickness of her legs and the size of her feet.

A big man of sullen countenance appeared in the door-way, ignored Carrie's visitor, and said to her, "I want you to go home and [look about that sow and the pigs]..." Carrie rolled up her knitting and got up. As the car left the curb Bob called, "hurry back, I'll be needing you here."

Credit: Library of Congress, Manuscript Division, WPA Federal Writers' Project Collection

Peggy is earning what Paddy is burning—a typical Irish home. Man, with holes in knees of pants, sits smoking pipe, and woman, standing in front of doorway, knitting. Keystone View Company, c. 1902.

Credit: Library of Congress, Prints & Photographs Division, reproduction #LC-USZ62-104769

Frogging My Engagement
by Dania Rajendra

Prologue

At Christmas, I was unemployed and flat broke. Blake and I had been together for almost four months. I thought about using my usual excuses for not buying presents for the winter gift-giving season—that I'm Hindu, Jewish, and leftist, I just don't *do* Christmas—but I didn't want to be a Scrooge. Also, things with us were feeling more and more momentous. Since Blake comes from a good Minnesotan Methodist family, I knew he'd get me something.

I was broke but was not without my yarn stash. And because I was unemployed, I had nothing but time. Our relationship was going so well that I didn't want to jinx it by making him a sweater—every knitting woman knows that to knit your boyfriend a sweater is to invite the end of your relationship. Plus, he'll walk off with your hours of hard work! I was twenty-four years old at the time and had been knitting since I was a ten-year-old. I learned from my mother, but I didn't become serious until I picked up my needles again in college. That's when I discovered what a haven a good local yarn store can be. Knitting my first sweater (seed stitch, with deep plum Lamb's Pride) kept me sitting still and able to focus on my history textbooks—somehow, knitting two and purling two gave my kinetic restlessness an outlet without requiring so much attention that I couldn't study. And when I needed to flee my history textbooks, I would walk the two miles down Grand Avenue to The Yarnery and immerse myself in the textures and colors.

For my Minnesotan, that Christmas some four years later, I made a pair of wool socks. They were cabled, white with navy stripes and heel and toe, to keep his feet warm through the winter.

We sat on the couch as he opened my gift. He looked over at me. He's a beautiful man with dark, thick hair and hazel eyes. His whole face softened when he saw the socks, and his eyes shone.

"It's the best Christmas present I've ever gotten," he said. "I can't believe you made them. You're so talented."

Watching him, I felt a rush of warmth in his chilly living room. I was relieved that he liked the socks so much, and I felt more confident in our relationship. Everything felt so right. We made love right there on the couch.

Two years later, we had moved in together, moved to New York, and gotten engaged. Blake is the uncle of three kids, and by this time I was consumed by my projects for them. I knit everywhere—on the subway, on my lunch break, and at my friends' dinner parties. For Christmas, the kids—Lili, four years old, and her sister Carmen, two years old, in Minnesota; and Connor, almost one year old, in Maryland—got hats with their names embroidered inside. After Christmas, I busied myself with a little sweater for Connor's first birthday in late January. It was blue with yellow stars and yellow raglan sleeves. I sent it to him with the Dr. Seuss book *Sneetches and Other Stories* and wrote the card about what a star kid he is—I love a good theme present. Next up was Lili's fifth birthday, in late February. It was mid-January. I had six weeks to knit some sort of gift for her.

Week One

We had plans to visit my best college buds in Boston, Katie and Marie, and their husbands, Jason and Sherman. Three of the four of them were in graduate school at Harvard, and they lived across the street from one another. I had sent them both IOUs for knitting lessons for Christmas. When they called the week before my scheduled visit to ask, "How are you?" I updated them with news of my projects: finished the mittens for my brother! Finished Connor's sweater, looking for the right buttons! It was easier to focus on that than tell the truth: I'm heartsick, I'm terrified, I'm working so hard to keep us together, and I don't think I can do it.

That week, I prepared my project for Lili. She was turning five years old, and her favorite colors were pink and purple. I decided I would plunge into uncharted territory for me: designing a sweater. It wasn't anything too difficult. I adapted a Debbie Bliss pattern for a basic ribbed sweater and plotted an "L" on the front and a "5" on the back. I spent afternoons in my cubicle reading knitty.com and taking long lunch breaks at the bookstore across the street from my office. After scanning the self-help shelves, desperate to find the book that contained the pattern for making an unhappy relationship a happy one, I bought Debbie Stoller's *Stitch 'N Bitch: A Knitter's Design Journal*. I brought it back to my office and pasted in a picture of Connor's star sweater so the book didn't seem so blank. That afternoon, I elbowed my fellow commuters for a seat on the subway. I then pored over graph paper, feverishly counting stitches, drawing, erasing, counting again, and redrawing until Lili's sweater looked perfect on paper.

Then, I translated the drawing into written instructions. I was ready to knit.

That Friday night, Blake and I took the express Chinatown bus to Boston. I knit the whole way in the dark so that the little light over my head wouldn't upset his sleep. I wore my Ganesha pendant, in the hope that the elephant god would remove obstacles. I prayed Blake would stay asleep, so that maybe he wouldn't be obviously grumpy, hostile, or mean over the weekend.

We got into Boston late, slept in on Saturday morning, and had brunch with our friends. That afternoon, Katie, Marie, and I left the guys piled on the couch watching the pre-game show. We took the Red Line to the nearest yarn store. As we walked down the steps from the sharp cold into the warm, cozy shop, I thought about my friends. I wouldn't have pegged Katie as a knitter. She's not particularly crafty, and not into the hand-made aesthetic. But a grad school colleague had taught her how to knit (but not to purl—hence the promise of lessons), and she was good at it. Most things come naturally to her, so it wasn't a surprise that knitting did, too. She was already stuck on her second garter stitch scarf and so bored she couldn't get through it. I suggested she try socks, on four needles, to crank up the challenge.

Marie was also a novice, but she liked to sew, and it didn't surprise me that she also wanted to learn to knit. At the yarn shop, she picked out some fuzzy angora in bright colors for a scarf.

The three of us had been friends for almost a decade. It was fun, but a little unsettling, to share knitting with them. For some reason, until now, knitting had felt like mine alone.

I roamed the store, looking at all the purple yarns, and made my selection—Debbie Bliss Merino and some Durex shimmer for the "L" and the "5." The total was $76. I hesitated as I looked at the cards in my wallet. Blake did the budget, and we often fought about money. I didn't want to pay with my check card and have the payment be rejected in front of my friends; I didn't want Blake to blame a bounced check on my $76 at the yarn store. I handed over my credit card and touched my Ganesha pendent. It rang through. My friends bought their needles and their yarn, and we headed home.

We walked into Katie and Jason's apartment with our bags, shucked our coats, and sat down to wind our skeins into balls. Jason and Sherman were interested to see and touch the yarn.

"It's so cool," said Sherman. "It's string, and you're going to make it into cloth." He reached over and hugged Marie. "It's so cool you're learning to do that."

"Thanks, sweetie, but you're messing up my ball." He handed it over reluctantly, and we asked him jokingly if he wanted his own needles.

"Men knit, too," I said. Blake rolled his eyes.

"Look, honey," I said to the back of his head. "I got the yarn for Lili's sweater. It's purple, her favorite color."

He turned to look me in the face. "It's nice. How much?"

"Eighty—I charged it."

"Why did you do that?!" He hissed. I faced him, feeling our friends' embarrassment, as well as my own. I took a deep breath, tried to keep my features from showing my emotion, and remembered our therapy techniques for dif-fusing conflict. I counted to ten silently.

"Honey," I said. "Why don't we talk about it later?" He gave me another look and then turned back to the game. I exhaled.

It wasn't even half-time, so Katie, Marie, and I set-tled in on the other couch. I sat between them, making a sample, taking the time to check the gauge, pausing to show them how to cast on, how to hold the yarn, watch-ing, correcting, and answering questions. It was great to feel competent, like an expert. Blake was ten years older than me, and with a decade more of life experience, he felt comfortable critiquing most of my techniques—my driv-ing, my cooking, my methods of budgeting, the way I trained our puppy, the way I folded his shirts, and the way I washed dishes. But as I sat there, I felt like Queen of the Knitters. I knew how to knit, purl, cable, change colors... and no one here could correct me.

Jason looked over at us from the other couch. "How did you learn to knit, Dania, did your grandma teach you?"

"No, my grandma was a great sewer, but she didn't knit. My mom taught me," I said. "She learned in Portugal—she biked all over Europe, and when she was in Portugal someone else's grandma taught her. That's why I knit Continental style," I said. "I mean, why," I said, turning to Katie, "I hold the yarn in my left hand, instead of the way Liz taught you." I showed her how. After a few minutes of intense concentration, Katie said, "It's faster."

Blake glanced over. "You guys should watch out," he told Jason and Sherman. "Dania's psycho about the knitting—she's addicted." I looked down at my swatch, stung. I thought back to when my knitting was something he thought was cool, unusual, and a talent. I remembered the socks. I tried to think of something smart-ass to say back, but my eyes swam, so I pretended to count the rows on the swatch. Out of the corner of my eye, I saw Marie put down her knitting as she carefully jerked her nascent scarf all the way to the back of the needles, so careful not to drop a stitch. I felt her and Katie's arms around my back.

That night, I had finished my swatch, hit the right gauge, and started the actual sweater. The six of us played poker at the dining table. I knit and played at the same time, gulping red wine, desperate for the weekend to be over. I did pretty well at the game, at least for a while, but then Blake figured out my strategy and took me down.

"You're so stupid," he said as he pulled the pile of chips toward his body. He refused to lend me chips. I refilled my wine glass and knit faster, more intently.

Week Two

We returned to New York on Sunday. On Monday, I was signed up to take a finishing class at a yarn store in Chelsea. I rushed out of work and schlepped through the sleety city to get there on time. I crowded around a table at the back of the store with about ten other knitters, all women. I was the youngest by at least five, and maybe ten, years. The shop was cold—the building must have turned the heat off after 5:00 PM. The teacher was a knitwear designer who sometimes taught at the Fashion Institute of

Technology (FIT). Her work was beautiful, her instructions confusing, and her manner impatient.

"You should all be leaving one knit stitch at each end of the row for selvedge," she told us. After a burst of questions, she backed up to explain seaming and define selvedge.

"Don't you know how to sew?" she asked us. We shook our heads sadly, and she looked at us disapprovingly. Soon I was whispering help to the women seated on either side of me and comparing my samples to theirs. I began to space out, and my mind returned to trying to unknot the problem of Blake and me. I started to invent little vignettes about my classmates, especially those who did not wear wedding rings. The stories were dark and depressing—I projected my future onto them, and it wasn't pretty. In the cold yarn shop, I longed to be home knitting under the covers with my dog snuggled up to me and my cold feet on my fiancé. I resolved, once again, to try to thaw the chill between us that the hissing radiators couldn't warm.

In the days that followed, knitting became even more central to getting through my time with Blake. We would sit in front of the TV, watching garbage, not talking. I would knit to tune out the stupid show and the awful silence between us. Eventually, he'd turn off the TV and head to bed.

"I just need to finish this row," I'd tell him. I'd wait until he was probably asleep, then crawl into bed and be careful not to wake him. I'd lie there, remembering when he would reach for me in his sleep. Now, I was glad to have our dog snuggled between us.

Week Three

It was our habit to take the train together in the morning. I knit while standing, with my ball in a bag dangling from my wrist and my purse on the floor between my feet. We kept the joint commuting up even when we had nothing to say to each other—or when we were fighting.

"Sorry," I'd interrupt him. "Hang on, I need to count the stitches." It shut him up. I felt victorious, mean, and small. I counted rows I didn't need to count.

Week Four

I had a business trip to San Francisco. I packed my project for Lili, bought a plane-safe yarn cutter, and printed out the TSA regulations that specifically allow knitting needles on airplanes. I knit through the meetings I had come to San Francisco to attend. I only had the sleeves of the sweater left to finish, and I decided to ration the rest of the pattern so I would have enough to do on the long flight back.

I had one afternoon off, and I spent it wandering around Chinatown, which was decorated for Chinese New Year. I poked into shop after shop just to look around, mindful of Blake and our never-ending fights about the budget. But in one store, the bags were on sale. I love purses—all shapes and colors. I bought a small tote and an even smaller purse—perfect for my project and for all the supplies: the little calculator I'd bought in the airport to work out the increases, the plane-safe yarn cutter, the cable needles, and the stitch markers. The two bags were $15—a New Year's special. I was hugely pleased and ready to justify my purchase once I got home.

On the plane home, I thought about the letter I would write to Lili to accompany the sweater. It would be a graphic novel, complete with drawings and stickers and pictures. It would tell the story of her sweater. I would explain how her sweater began as yarn and paste in a photograph of it partially knitted. I would tell her how her sweater flew on an airplane, and visited San Francisco, and celebrated Chinese New Year. I would get Blake to take a picture of me knitting on the subway and tell her that's how Uncle Blake and Aunt Dania go to work every day, instead of in a car like her Daddy does. The project grew bigger than the knitting—it had to because the counting and the designing couldn't drown out the obvious truth: Uncle Blake and Aunt Dania weren't going to make it to the altar.

Week Five

I got back to a big work deadline, worked a thirteen-hour day, and stopped at the post office to pick up a box printed with balloons to send Lili her sweater. I came home to a dark apartment and an angry fiancé. We had a huge fight, in which Blake once again listed all my shortcomings. I twisted my ring, exhausted and clear on the fact that we had reached the end.

I left that weekend, while he was away on business. Katie and Marie came down from Boston to help and to take me back with them so I could recuperate from a distance. They brought the red wine, and I packed in a tipsy frenzy: throwing dirty laundry into a suitcase, grabbing favorite books, stuffing my jewelry box and favorite sentimental items in a box. I dumped my knitting baskets—the needles, the entire yarn stash, and Lili's sweater, which was in finished parts, ready to be blocked and seamed—into a bag.

Week Six

I spent a week in Boston. I was dry-eyed as I dismantled our life together. I had the diamond dug out of my engagement ring, I changed email passwords, opened a new bank account, and gave him the dog.

He called me two or three times a day that week. He also sent me emails with subject lines like "coming clean," in which he wrote, "I understand my behavior comes out of my unhappiness. I've been too afraid to tell you that I was scared; I know now that was wrong." He begged me to reconsider. I was calm, but once I'd snapped the phone closed, I'd sob in big, noisy gulps. Somewhere in the middle of one of those conversations, he asked me not to send Lili the sweater.

I recruited Marie, whose futon I was sleeping on that week, to help me frog it. She sat across from me, and the sweater pieces were between us like a dismembered doll. She let me wail as she pulled the yarn. When we were done, I was all cried out. I sat surrounded by mounds of kinky, purple yarn. I shoved it, unwound, back into the bag with the rest of my stash.

When I returned to New York, I stayed with my friend Erica and her husband. The previous year, I had taught Erica to knit, and in that one year, she had knit more garments, and more complicated garments, than I had in my sixteen years as a knitter. She was a maniac—and an inspiration. I knew she wouldn't mind that I soaked the purple yarn in her bathroom sink and hung it to dry from her shower curtain rod. I pored through her knitting books and magazines. I slept with them on the pull-out couch in her living room.

Erica went through the patterns with me, interspersing "You deserve better" and "You'll make it" and "You should be with someone who likes you happy" into our conversation about what project to start next. I finally settled on a pair of complicated, twisting, braided cable gloves. I thought the intricate pattern would distract me, but I could barely remember how to make a cable. I couldn't count the stitches. I couldn't even make a gauge sample. I ripped the first glove out and started a different project. I sat with the knitting in my lap and stared into space.

Six Months Later...

That purple yarn is still in my stash bag, half-straightened and neatly wound, half a big, kinky mess. I've earmarked it for projects to benefit a shelter for battered women.

A few months ago, I made a sweater for myself. It's called "Candy," a pattern I found on knitty.com. I made it in purple with orange stripes. I added Lili's Durex shimmer to the stripes. The sweater was the first thing I made for myself since I completed those Christmas socks for Blake.

I finished it after another one of those thirteen-hour workdays. I was in an empty bar in Brooklyn, waiting on my new boyfriend. He was late. I sipped Jameson's and worked in the ends. When Jonathan got to the bar, he rushed over to take my hand. "I'm so, so, so sorry." he said, his blue eyes widening. "I got stuck on the train..." He stopped mid-explanation to admire the sweater and ask me to model it. The Durex glinted in the low light. The sweater is very snug, a fact he noted appreciatively. He bought my drink, picked up my bag, and took me home to make me dinner. He has since asked for a sweater of his own. I explained the curse, but I'm looking around for a good pattern.

"End of the Day." Elderly woman and man knitting and reading. Created c. 1917, October 10.
   Credit: Library of Congress, Prints & Photographs Division, reproduction #LC-USZ62-55801

BELIEVING IN SOCKS
BY LELA NARGI

It is a blustery Vermont winter afternoon, grimly lit and loud with the noise of windows chattering in their casings. I am sitting cross-legged in the middle of the bed with needles, yarn, and pattern spread before me. I read the pattern for socks once, then again, then picked up the needles and yarn and begin to knit. The awkwardness of four slim double-pointeds dispersed among my fingers fades away after a few rounds, leaving my mind free to skip around other subjects. I think idly of the raw dinner ingredients awaiting conclusion in the fridge, an email I forgot to send to a friend, the waning balance of my bank account. These are the usual musings of my days, banal for all their pessimistic potential (Will I burn the stew? Will the friend be angry? Will my family end up homeless?). The answers, of course are: no, no, and definitely no. And there is banality, too, in my desire to conjure drama where little exists so that I can rationalize it away, back to the realm of the... banal.

After a half hour of this sort of mini-crisis-creation-and-management, I discover that with the movement of the yarn, my thoughts have become stuck in a groove. Over and over, I am reciting a sentence from an essay by Joan Didion: "We are here on this island in the middle of the Pacific in lieu of filing for divorce."

It is almost Christmas, and I am knitting socks, my first socks, for my husband. I am knitting them in secret, squirreled away in the bedroom with the door shut in case he should arrive home while I'm at it. In defiance of my usual, casual dabblings in the provinces of pessimism, I am knitting the socks as a grand token of optimism. As for the secret, it has little to do with the fact that I intend these socks to be a gift and so wish them to remain under wraps until Christmas morning. Rather, I am not yet willing to let on to another soul that I could, in any way, concede to this optimism.

"I am here with this yarn in the middle of my bed in lieu of filing for divorce." This variation enters my head and stays there until it is time to attend to those dinner ingredients—a quick browning of meat in the stockpot, additions of chopped vegetables and herbs and broth, in preparation for a long simmer. Afterward, I return to my bedroom island, and the sock, and my thoughts—or thought.

"I am here with this yarn . . ." It sounds, in view of my very immediate circumstances, like a hopeful beginning. To be snug in this room while outside it is twelve below and brittle with wind is in itself a cause for delight. And to be alone in the company of yarn and several open-ended hours is further reason to celebrate.

". . . in lieu of filing for divorce." Despite the bite of the ultimate word, the latter half of the sentence sounds hopeful too, in this moment. I am doing this—knitting socks—instead of doing that—filing for divorce.

I'm not sure if I'm relieved or annoyed when it comes time at last to turn the heel and instructions for intervals of decreasing—back to the banal—take over my consciousness. I've been reciting the line without cease, but I'm no closer to determining whether my optimism is warranted. Because what I really want is to believe that my marriage can be saved by the simple act of knitting a pair of socks.

Reading the idea as I write it here on paper, it seems preposterous, a dangerous flight of fancy our therapist, should I have presented it to her, might have cautioned was an avoidance of the real work at hand: learning to listen, learning to listen with our hearts, learning to truly hear each other's pain. I must be conscious of this; after all, I am knitting in secret, sharing my optimistic frill with no one. Still, sitting on my down-soft bed as winter clatters all around, and grey and red alpaca threads through my fingers, over needle points, and into an orderly tube, there is a glint for the first time in months. A glint of the possible. These socks could be the answer to everything.

It is a late afternoon in late December, and the aroma of stew permeates my refuge, an invisible barrier against the vagaries of blustering winter. The first sock is almost ready for bind-off. A glow of nostalgia for such a smell on a cold day, and the touch of yarn in my hands, and the anticipation of giving a gift that has been made even with cautious intention, settles over me. It is redolent of happy Christmases past, of a time before the advent of true and lingering pessimism, when this composite sensation of well-being seemed the norm, not an aberration. It is a late December afternoon, and I am knitting under the influence of my secret optimism. Socks can solve the muddles of marriage. The impulse to knit these particular socks is an incontrovertible act of affection and therefore, surely, must be a beacon of the end of unhappiness.

What I don't know on this late December afternoon is that on a morning in early January, I will shrink the socks. They will have been given and received on Christmas morning with all the desired joyfulness and enthusiasm of spirit. They will have been worn three times, three days in a row by my husband, each time accompanied by exclamations regarding their comfort and snugness of fit. They will have been discovered, by me, at the bottom of a basket of dirty laundry. As pants and shirts and tights and napkins churned beside me in a bath of warm suds, I will have held up the socks, slightly stretched now, one in each hand, and debated with myself for long minutes: Did I knit these socks out of machine-washable yarn? No.

Should I drop them in the wash anyway? No. Yes. No.

What will happen if I wash them in the machine? They will shrink.

Will they really? Yes. No. Yes. No. No. Yes.

Did I knit these socks so that I could wash them by hand every week? No.

Does it even occur to him that they have to be washed by hand? No. Yes. No. It should. No, it shouldn't. Yes, it should. He's not a knitter—why should it?

Anyway, why should I be the one to wash these socks? For the same reason—whatever *that* is—that I am the one who always attends to all the wash, the meals, the budget.

Why should I be the one to wash these socks? I shouldn't. I should tell him they need to be washed by hand and let him wash them himself. No, I shouldn't—that would be petty. The real driving force of the last two years of our marriage—pettiness. Then, what should I do?

Drop the socks in the wash. See what happens.

You know what happens. The socks will emerge from the washing machine several sizes smaller—actually, due to my uneven knitting, one sock will be two sizes smaller; the other sock about four, tight as armor and well-felted. I will howl and weep over them as if it had never occurred to me that such a thing could have occurred. By the time I present the ruined socks to my husband, I will be utterly convinced of my ignorance about the matter. I want to believe I am kinder than this.

"I'm so sorry," I will cry. "I had no idea they would shrink!"

He will accept this as truth; I will feel shame and pessimism for the fate of our marriage in such a climate as we have created, and also uncertainty about the wisdom of having ascribed the power of optimism to an article of knitwear.

Back there in December, though, I know nothing of any of this. As the scant light fades further and the wind settles, and the stew softens, I cast on for the second sock. After a few rounds, I catch myself reciting again: "I am here with this yarn in the middle of my bed in lieu of filing for divorce." I won't tell a soul, but I believe it.

Mothers, Daughters, & Granddaughters

THE CASTLE OF OUR DREAMS
BY KATIE BENEDICT

When I was ten years old, my mother, finding no other means of employment, took a job as caregiver for a ninety-three-year-old woman named Mrs. Lane. Mother had divorced my father nine years earlier, and we never saw a penny of child support over the years. Eventually, my mother and I sought solace in the sanctuary of her parents' home. Nevertheless, our money quickly dwindled, and job opportunities were slim during the early 1980s in our rural Alabama town.

Mother's hours with Mrs. Lane extended beyond any regular factory shifts or union regulations. When she accepted the position, she committed all of her nights as well as three days a week, with no holidays. The strenuous schedule drained my mother quickly, aging her before my young eyes. She'd sit awake most nights in Mrs. Lane's musty old house, watching after the elderly woman and tending to her needs. Then she would come home exhausted to face the boundless energy of a lonely and hyperactive little girl, as well as the increasing demands of her own aging parents.

Her obligations left no room for hobbies or social activities. Instead, she hoarded precious hours of sleep whittled out while I was in school and her parents were resting. When I barreled through the door each afternoon, she'd awaken, bleary yet once again eager to indulge my childhood lunacies. But most of her time trickled past in idle conversations with elderly ladies or mute hours of forced camaraderie, hostage to soap operas and sitcoms.

Occasionally, on those nights my grandparents felt particularly unwell and couldn't endure another evening of my antics, I'd accompany my mother to Mrs. Lane's house. She'd hustle me into the dusty back bedroom where Mrs. Lane's daughter once slept and played decades before, a little girl who had died over a quarter-century ago. An ancient black-and-white television teetered on a tiny corner table, and piles of neglected *National Geographic* magazines hovered along one wall, ready in case I became bored with my books and transistor radio.

I usually behaved well in Mrs. Lane's house; something calm and silent exuded from the patched antique furniture and the piles of pennies that were stacked everywhere. The pennies were remnants of the eccentric Mr. Lane, who'd passed away five years earlier. Sleep often eluded me on the nights I spent in the daughter's bed, which was a creaky antique. Midnight stretched wearily into dawn as I lay awake, feigning sleep while I listened to music or thumbed magazine pages by flashlight, ignoring the phantoms lurking just shy of my vision.

I can't remember the exact day, but sometime during the course of a restless spring evening, Mrs. Lane gave to my mother more than the meager salary we so dearly needed. One night, sitting on a decrepit sofa in front of the television and watching the episodes of *Guiding Light* Mother had videotaped for her, Mrs. Lane taught my mother to knit. The two women had become bored with their tedious lives and with each other; they'd already said all they had to say, shared all the stories they could recall. At some point, their conversation had touched on a pastime that Mrs. Lane had once enjoyed years ago when her eyes were sharp and her hands were steady. She spoke to my mother of patterns and blankets and Fair Isle sweaters to bundle babies during brisk autumn football games. Mother listened and imagined me swaddled in tiny, even stitches.

The next day, Mother drove to Wal-Mart and bought a skein of cheap, yellow yarn and two aluminum needles. She plopped the parcel proudly into Mrs. Lane's lap. Mrs. Lane was pleased with the unexpected diversion, and she took up her own needles once again. Her fingers trembled as she twisted an end of yarn into loops and instinctively began to cast on stitches. Mother drew the other end of the ball into her own hands and patiently mimicked Mrs. Lane's motions with her needles. She quietly asked questions and ripped back awkward loops, while the older woman explained each step and taught her the rhyme she'd learned very long ago:

"Jump through your loop, slip under the track (that's the needle, dear), grab a lamb, bring him all the way back."

I wasn't present for that first lesson, but I lay on the floor of Mrs. Lane's living room on many subsequent evenings. I watched by the flicker of the TV as my mother lounged alongside a snoozing Mrs. Lane and completed row after yellow row of uneven garter stitch, then miles of stockinette. Finally, the glorious moment arrived when she leaned down and handed me the ugliest length of fabric I'd ever seen.

"It's a scarf!" she assured me. "I made you a scarf!"

I wasn't sure what to do with it—there was no chance I'd wrap that haggard tangle of yarn around my neck; I accepted her offering with a smile of encouragement and put it to use as a coaster under my soda that night. Morning found it slightly sticky and sodden with dark, syrupy stains, so I shoved it inside a magazine where it was pressed between pictures of South American butterflies.

With so much time to spend knitting, my mother soon announced she needed a Project. One Saturday, she left home early in the morning and canvassed every Wal-Mart, K-Mart, and Big Lots in the county. She triumphantly returned home with a thin pattern book and seven bags bursting with multi-hued acrylic yarn. Her face beamed with exhilaration as she opened the book to a dog-eared page and stabbed her finger at the picture she'd carefully chosen.

There, splayed over the page in absurdly vivid colors, gleamed the most sensational representation of a castle that I'd ever seen. Depicted in a glossy full-page photo, the intricately knit motif crept across the entire blanket and wrapped the four-poster bed on which it lay in a frenzy of color and fantasy that would delight any child. Gold and brown turrets twined into a turquoise sky swept with white cotton candy clouds. A moat divided the base of the castle from emerald, flower-speckled meadows spanning the horizon. Staring at the fairy castle, I envisioned a dragon splashing in the moat and a knight galloping up the hill that loomed in the distance. My imagination soared with glorious possibilities. This was my very own castle, my haven, and my mother would build it for me, stitch by stitch. With no hesitation, Mother and I dove into the sea of yarn, tossing colors into various piles and double-checking that we had enough to complete the pattern. Although the yarn was inexpensive and coarse, I'm sure the sheer number of skeins the pattern required drained every extra penny of my mother's paycheck that week.

Mother anxiously skimmed the instructions while I reclined in a sea of yarn, dreaming of my acrylic castle. Within an hour, she completed four squares of sky and labored over a complex half moat/half meadow miter square. I curled up at her side, embellishing the pattern with colored pencils, drawing a princess with flowing hair and azure eyes gazing from the tower window.

That night, due to a rare visit from Mrs. Lane's grand-daughter, Mother didn't have to go to work. After my grandparents retired to their bed, she pulled me onto the sofa beside her, handed me an extra set of needles she'd bought, and pulled a skein of fluffy pink yarn from her pocketbook. I sat at her side, and slowly she helped me twist the yarn in my hands, repeating the rhyme Mrs. Lane had taught her months ago:

"Jump through your loop, slip under the track, grab a lamb, bring him all the way back."

In no time, I caught on and filled our laps with clouds of knitted pink acrylic. I sat perched happily beside my mother as she churned out squares of gold and honey and the green grass mingled with blue sky and brick road. Our needles looped together a night that burns in my memory, not for its significance, but for the comfortable solidarity we shared building our private castle while my mother's other charges slept.

Throughout June, my mother hauled yarn everywhere, and the piles of completed squares multiplied: thirty-seven turquoise, forty-eight emerald, ten honey. I counted our inventory nightly, thrilled with the colors and lost in my imaginary kingdom. While my grandparents ranted about their pains and ailments, Mother clucked and clinked her needles sympathetically. When Mrs. Lane snored in front of the television with dinner cold in her lap, Mother turned down the lights and settled into a pile of yarn. As she waited for me to come home from school, Mother's fingers danced their now-familiar rhythm.

For a while, I enjoyed our ritual, clinging to princess dreams as I knit through the long nights I spent at Mrs. Lane's house with Mother. My sleepovers had become more frequent as my grandmother battled debilitating bouts of pneumonia throughout the spring. Yarn and needles whirling, I was too busy to notice the house's creepy penny piles and the shadows that snarled on the floor. I didn't mind the hard, sour treats Mrs. Lane often pressed secretly into my palm. In the gloomy back bedroom, my pink yarn took on a life of its own. It morphed at my touch into a shimmering veil, a royal sash, an exotic turban. I was finally able to sleep in that dreary house, exhausted by my efforts, dreaming of kingdoms, and horses, and princes.

In time, my grandmother healed, and I no longer accompanied my mother to the Lane house at all. The twilit evenings lengthened, and I toyed with my pink yarn. I missed our moments huddling with our heads together and giggling over skipped stitches while Mrs. Lane slept. The restoration of my solitude tarnished the novelty of Mother's hobby. In my own familiar bed, I could not find the excitement in crouching under a blanket and knitting frantically through the wee hours of morning. Without my partner's vigilance, my own desire to knit faded, and my interest in the castle dwindled.

July arrived, and without the diversion of school, empty hours of hot Southern days stretched eternally. I wandered, searching for something elusive, impatient in the dusk of my childhood. The days limped along and the restlessness of my youth propelled me into the twisted arms of mimosa tress, then farther from home, through desolate construction yards and abandoned lots. Back at home, under my bed, forlorn yards of pink, fluffy yarn gathered dust.

I craved companionship. But families with children eschewed our remote location. Of the few neighbors residing near us, only one had a child, a girl of five, who was far too young to be an adequate playmate. My grandparents indulged me occasionally but secretly sighed with relief when I tired of their limited entertainment and ducked outside, leaving them to smoke cigarettes and meander together through their ruminations. Meanwhile, my mother continued to obsess over her mountains of yarn and visions of castles, oblivious to my increased isolation.

By August, her hobby infuriated me. I'd never known my mother to possess a passion for something other than me. Growing up an only child in an exclusively adult environment spoiled me in many ways, yet deprived me of something essential: a network of my peers. I longed for attention and desired to be the focus of my mother's concentration. The now unwelcome distraction of a knitted castle tickled my resentment, and I fumed in shadows while she hummed in quiet contentment, her fingers flying.

My growing rage blinded me to the truth: that my mother's intentions all still focused on me. Her hobby was not her own; every stitch she drew with her needles was constructed for me. My mother was doing more than creating a warm blanket or passing the time. With every loop of yarn, she labored to feed my dreams through the only tools she possessed. Her hands callused from the scrape of abrasive fibers over soft flesh, but she hardly felt the burn. The time reserved for precious sleep, once so eagerly hoarded, diminished as the castle grew stitch by stitch. Caught up in the bliss of creating enchantment for her only daughter, Mother missed my haunted stares and saw instead only the rapture that had flooded my features the night she showed me pictures of the blanket. If she could just build the fiber fortress quickly enough, she might lock us inside that magical moment, capturing our happiness forever.

One long, lazy day I found Mother rocking gently on the front porch swing and racing through squares faster by the minute. I vaulted into her lap, hungry for attention. But my enthusiastic scramble caused her to hurl yarn and needles in all directions. A scowl darkened Mother's face as she shooed me away while she salvaged her supplies. Her chiding words chased me out of the yard and into the field beside our house.

Shamed by my blunder, I set out to win her forgiveness and maybe a few minutes of her time. All afternoon I practiced my penitence, collecting recyclable aluminum cans we could compact and exchange at the local grocery for "mad money." Once my bags were full of dripping beer cans, I plucked a handful of Black-Eyed Susans and scooped up a seven-toed kitten I'd stumbled across drinking rusty water from a ditch. No one could ignore those ministrations! But dusk surprised me. I raced fireflies though the magnolia night, sprinting under an orange-ribboned sky. I arrived home, panting, to find that my mother had already gone to work. Reeking of spilled beer, I collapsed on the front step and dissolved into tears beside the small howling kitten. In that moment, all my loneliness and childhood torment focused on a new enemy. I was angry with my mother, but my resentment turned to her Project. I raged against her yarn and her needles. And above all, I hated her castle.

Mother returned home the next morning to chaos. By daybreak, neighborhood dogs had scattered the aluminum cans across our driveway and garden. The bouquet of wildflowers had withered on the porch swing, and the kitten had peed all over the kitchen floor. Mother was perplexed by the odd circumstances she discovered, yet she was also eternally efficient. She quickly set matters right by gathering piles of cans and feeding the pitifully mewing cat before settling in to complete a few more squares of sky and clouds before the day began in earnest and more pressing duties interfered.

I woke late that morning. My eyes were crusted with night tears, and my small body was drenched in sweat from the summer heat. Stumbling into the living room, still clad only in my damp cotton gown, I discovered Mother on the couch with her knitting needles in hand and the new kitten curled serenely on her lap. The crinkly lines that had lately spread across her features relaxed as she turned another square with satisfaction. I'd passed the prior night wrenching my pillow with sobs of genuine desolation and sleeping only when exhaustion overcame my pain. My mother's blatant happiness bore into my soul, and I wanted to shriek at her betrayal. I was only a child, after all, and had spent far too many frustrating days in the company of my stoic, invalid grandparents. The perplexing hormones of adolescence crept into my veins, confusing my emotions, and stoking my temper. I knew only that for too many hours, I played alone.

In retrospect, I plead that I was victim to the instability of pre-pubescence. I caved in to my hormonal haze and in a breathtaking display of ignorance, I erupted into a tantrum of paramount proportions. She had not even woken me that morning! Had not even waited to say goodbye the prior night before leaving! I trembled with my own insignificance. Storming barefoot across the carpet, I gathered handfuls of knitted squares in my arms and flung them across the room. Tears streamed down my face as my hands grappled for skeins of yarn. I don't remember finding the pattern and shredding it, but weeks later I discovered ragged fragments of turret and meadow peeking out from under a corner of carpet.

Mother froze mid-stitch. She was astonished at my explosion and motionless, until my fingers sought hers and yanked her project from her hands. She'd underestimated the impact of her simple pursuit on our relationship. She hadn't noticed the subtle changes that were turning her little girl into a young woman before her unseeing eyes. She overlooked my vulnerability and assumed that my longing for a fairyland castle matched her own. She thought it would be obvious that our castle, her time, was all for me.

Although I could not understand, it was always for me.

Finally, she saw me: She noticed for the first time that summer the pimples that dotted my forehead and the way my arms and legs had grown beyond the boundaries of my clothing. Witnessing my silent torment, she realized that the price of our castle had been too high after all. That hot summer morning, Mother put down her needles and gathered my tense, sweaty body into her arms. She whispered words of comfort through our sobs. In the afternoon, she packed away the yarn, the needles, and the perfect little squares. As the long, sultry days dwindled toward autumn, we spent our time playing games and dolls. We squeezed out every minute together that we could. Neither of us mentioned the castle again.

When I think back on that last summer of my childhood, I wonder if it was that morning of anger that triggered my spiral into adolescence. In September, I turned eleven years old and got my period a month later. Because of new zoning restrictions, I was bused to a new school in town. My new school was lacking in funds, but to my excitement, it was bursting with students. I made friends and no longer had to depend upon my mother for entertainment. I grew up fast after that and never stopped to look back. Within a year, I kissed a boy and smoked a cigarette. By the following summer, I juggled a harried social life, and time to spend with my mother was a low priority.

But the death of Mrs. Lane the following April forced Mother down a bleaker employment path anyway. Working the graveyard shift at the local chicken processing factory left her so exhausted, she barely noticed my dubious friends and increasingly wild behavior. I no longer sought time alone with her, which was just as well since she had none to give.

As far as I know, she never again had time to give a thought to the castle made of yarn that had once captivated our fantasies.

Twenty years later finds us worlds away from everything that transpired that summer. Thousands of miles and years of misunderstandings separate my mother and me. We speak often but somehow never touch on the topic of hazy Alabama days, or nights of stolen giggles in the back parlor of a sleeping old woman's house. We certainly ignore the difficult years that followed that summer and the excruciating season of my stumble toward maturity.

Then there came a day, not long ago, that I clenched two knitting needles against my palms once again. They were hard and cold and familiar. A friend handed them to me with a ball of lavender yarn, then prompted my fingers to twine and twist a strand of wool until it emerged from my hands as a very ugly scarf. Until then, I'd not touched yarn or needles since my tenth summer, always recalling my eventual, lingering distaste for the experience. But as a gesture of friendship to an eager pal, here I was learning once again to knit. With the touch of the aluminum, memories of the forsaken castle flooded over me, excruciating even after so much time and space.

I knit my second, slightly less ugly scarf and a pair of mittens and mailed them to my mother. Only after I was sure she'd received my package did I call to confess I'd learned to knit. My mother responded, "That's nice," then, "Has the weather turned cold up there yet?" Soon afterward, I completed an intricate forest green shawl and sent it for her birthday. I was excited again, but still apprehensive about how she might respond. After all these years, I was making a determined return to the hobby that had marked a poignant turning point in our relationship. She called to thank me for the shawl, but she mentioned nothing about our days of laughter and battles over castle squares.

As I continued to knit, my thoughts drifted incessantly to the marvelous castle that never came to be. Soon, it haunted my dreams, just as it had years ago during those discontented hours of my childhood. Tentatively at first, then with increased diligence, I rummaged collections of afghan patterns and scanned pages of Internet sites, seeking any reference to Mother's long-forgotten project. It appears to have vanished as completely as Brigadoon, leaving no trace save for the lingering image embedded firmly in my own mind.

Finally, one day as my mother and I once again chatted about absolutely nothing significant over the telephone, I drew a breath, mustered my courage, and said something

I hoped might bridge the years. I asked her about the fate of the castle I had grown to detest so much.

"That old thing?" she said after a moment's pause. "I haven't thought about that in years. I have no idea where it got to." Then she inquired about the weather again, reverting the conversation to the comfort of nothing at all.

I remembered how she'd loved her castle, how she'd caressed the lengths of rough yarn, and I batted back tears as I answered, "It's not supposed to rain until Wednesday. But the temperature might drop into the thirties tonight." And that was the end of it. Apparently, I'd succeeded in banishing the castle from her mind, not just for a summer but for a lifetime.

A month ago, I mailed my mother some needles and yarn, but she claimed to have forgotten how to knit and said she hadn't the time to learn. I offered to teach her again when I visited for Thanksgiving, but she clicked her tongue and told me there'd be snow on Saturday.

Last week, during that moment when both of us had nothing to say and were considering how we might end the call, Mother suddenly asked what it was that I was knitting and if I would bring some of my projects with me when I came home.

Of course, I agreed. I will bring everything. I will give her needles and skeins of fine merino and show her the way to form those tight little loops. I will coax her with fluffy yarns and irresistible patterns. We will sit together on the sofa with our heads bent together and our giggles breaking the night.

I have my own Project now. It's a mission to span the terrible gap I forged years ago and the gap Mother and I struggle to bridge with every conversation we have these days. If you catch me fumbling through boxes of mildewed yard sale patterns or purchasing vast amounts of Technicolor yarn, I'm sure you'll understand why.

It's time for me to rebuild my mother's castle.

Domestic Thrift—A study from real life—Ireland, 1904. Woman seated operating a spinning wheel outside a thatched-roof stone cottage as woman standing in cottage doorway knitting looks on. Carelton H. Graves, creator and publisher, Philadelphia.
Credit: Library of Congress Prints & Photographs Division, reproduction #LC-USZ62-123755

PATCHES
BY JANET ENGLE

I'm losing my grandmother a bit each day.

As pieces of her fade away and layers of her memories are unraveled by the fingers of Alzheimer's, there is so much to feel sorrow about. I regret that my children, nieces, and nephews will remember their grandmother as only a shell of her former self. I feel bad for my parents who, as her care-givers, plan their days around her needs. I sympathize with my aunt, who lives several hundred miles away from her mother and must make decisions about her care based on the opinions of others.

Of course, I feel bad for my grandmother. I can't even imagine what it must be like to be locked out of reality by your own mind.

But in my heart, I'm a selfish person. I mostly feel bad for myself, and what I truly mourn about Grandma's illness is the growing revelation that I never really knew this woman.

I know all kinds of things about her, of course. I know she was one of five girls and that her mother desperately wanted a boy. I know that she had a scholarship to a teacher's college but chose instead to marry and have a family. Because of a coal mining accident, she was a widow with two small children at twenty years old.

I know she attended all my school concerts and assemblies, teetering along in her brown leather, square-toed high heel shoes and always wearing a bright red wool jacket and skirt set, with a white polyester blouse adorned at the neck with a floppy bow.

I know she lost a toe to a lawn mower and won a battle against skin cancer, but still refused to get a new, safer, mower or wear sunscreen. She overcooked vegetables and undercooked oatmeal. She hoarded the new bath towels people brought as presents, preferring to use the old familiar ones with holes, but she considered a monthly perm an undeniable necessity.

I know a lot about my grandmother, but I don't know her.

I don't know how long she missed my grandfather, or if she was mad at him for dying. I don't know what her dreams for her life and her children's lives were, or if those dreams were ever accomplished or even voiced.

I don't know if she loved the mountains where she was born and lived her entire life, or if they were like a prison from which she longed to escape.

I don't even know what she loved, what she was passionate about, what she looked forward to doing every day.

I can't ask her anymore. If I hadn't been too busy with my own life, maybe I would have realized this before. Perhaps we could have sat with a pot of tea and the family photo albums and talked about what it was like to be a single mother in the 1940s and what she would have done differently if she had a chance.

By the time her illness was diagnosed, Grandma was unable to care for herself. She moved across the street with my parents, leaving her trailer available for visiting children and grandchildren. Her mobile home has become a time capsule, a museum. It seems as though my grandmother could step back into her home and life any minute. Her coffee pot still sits on the counter. Her toiletries are nestled in the bathroom cabinet—all the soaps, deodorants, and shampoos she bought in bulk at a discount, side by side with expired medicine. Her bedroom smells like face powder, fabric softener, and Wind Song. A bowl of plastic fruit with grapes so realistic that, as a child, I always had to squeeze to convince myself they weren't fresh, decorates the kitchen table.

The only thing that has changed are the bathroom towels. My mother threw out the rags and finally put up some of the nice ones Grandma was perpetually saving for "when she needed them."

Staying there one weekend, I decided I needed to find out about this woman who had been such a constant but mysterious part of my life. While the kids were tucked away in the bed where she used to sleep, and my husband tried to work up the courage to treat his headache with a nine-year-old aspirin, I scoured Grandma's bookcases and magazine cabinets, looking for some pattern, some signal of what was important to her.

The collection was eclectic to say the least—mementos and postcards from places she had never been, books of political essays that had never been opened, biographies of old movie stars, and romantic paperbacks with covers that made me blush. For one shining moment, selfish woman that I am, I was overcome with pride to see my graduation picture stashed among her treasures. The heady feeling was quickly dashed, however, when I came across an issue of *The National Enquirer* from the same year right under my photograph.

I still didn't know her. I didn't know her at all.

I found shopping lists and recipes, newspaper clippings, and books of stamps. I found instructions to a lot of fad diets and a cross carved from genuine olive wood from Jerusalem, guaranteed.

There had to be more to her than what I had found: souvenirs from other people's trips, celebrity gossip, and weight loss. I only had one pile left, and I was no closer to understanding my grandmother than before I started.

Then I found it: a well-worn, dog-eared copy of *Learn to Knit*. The cover was long gone, and the staples that held it together were rusted. Under this little instruction guide, there were other patterns and books for all different kinds of crafts, many with notes on gauges, materials, and intended purposes.

"Pretty with slacks, pink cotton?"

"Size 8 needles, do ribbing tight"

"Christmas present for Emil"

"Buy enough yarn for matching coasters"

She had knitting patterns for styles that spanned five decades. Digging through her stash of magazines, books, and pamphlets, I giggled at the pictures of knee-length sweaters with quarterback shoulders and huge blocks of neon. A little further down were pictures of miniskirts, ponchos, and berets—all in avocado and orange stripes. Then there were the black and white directions for a cotton baby layette, which were published the year before my father was born.

I remembered my grandmother knitting, but I hadn't realized how important the craft must have been to her. She always seemed to be working on a sweater, a scarf, or an afghan—often several projects at a time. Her finished work was unique and interesting, to describe it kindly. In particular, I remember a giant afghan she made out of individually knitted squares. Each block was a lovely shade of green, blue, or brown from her stash of scrap yarn. She worked on the pieces for over a year, knitting through morning talk shows and long waits at the doctor's office.

When the squares were finally finished and she joined them together, she ended up with a pucker between each corner of every single square. Rather than pulling out the joins and trying a different method, she whip-stitched a circle of hot pink flannel over each pucker.

She chose hot pink because that's what she had on hand.

My life has been very different from my grandmother's. I went to college, left the mountains, and haven't worn high heels in at least fifteen years. I grew up just across the street from her, but not much of Grandma seemed to have rubbed off on me. Knowing that my time with her was growing shorter, I wanted to find some common ground with this woman. I wanted to feel that even after she died, part of her would live on in me.

So, I learned to knit. I could not bring myself to learn from the same book she had. My grandmother had written notes on nearly every page of her little manual. My eyes would fall on the sure, steady handwriting from her youth, and I would remember how she struggled now just to print her first name.

I found it impossible to knit while crying, so I found my own *Learn to Knit* kit from the local craft store and persevered until the diagrams made sense and the stitches didn't seem like impossible magic.

Halfway through my first scarf, I became bored by the monotony of the garter stitch. I remembered that my grandmother seldom finished a project before moving to a new one. This helped me to conquer my own tendencies to plow through and finish something no matter how much I hate it. I came to accept that the joy of knitting can be in the process, not necessarily in getting to the finish line quickly. At least, that's how I justified it to myself.

I started a triangular, rice-stitch shawl and saved my simple scarf to work on during long car rides.

Eventually, I finished that garter-stitch scarf. My thrill at completing a project turned to disappointment when I realized that knitting in the dark while traveling down the highway and singing along to the classic rock station was not the recipe for high-quality results. Even the most aggressive blocking couldn't straighten out my wobbly, uneven edges.

On a whim, my first experience with knitting turned into my first experiment with felting. After only ten minutes in the washing machine, months of work was reduced to a short, thick, inflexible, strip of fabric. A few nips with the scissors on alternating sides of the piece and I had created a "unique and interesting" garment of my own.

That was the moment I knew my grandmother. That is when I saw her in me.

Other people might fix bad stitches or purchase coordinating fabric before covering puckers. They might unravel a wavy-edged scarf and reuse the wool, or pack the pitiful thing away so they could later see how much they had improved.

Not my grandmother and me. We are both jumpers. We would rather deal with our mistakes quickly, if not particularly *well*. Other people weigh their options, make informed decisions, and would be mortified at ruining months of work on a whim.

We would rather be moving on to the next project and not dwelling on the last one.

Even though she lives three hundred miles away, I feel closer to my grandmother than ever before because each time I pick up my needles, I think of her. I don't obsess about her illness and what has been lost to me already. I resist the urge to regret the years I was too busy to have that pot of tea with her.

Instead, I think of how she did the exact same stitches I do now. She knit. She purled. She got in a groove and on good days marveled at how quickly and easily a garment grew. She felt frustrated and infuriated at fingers and needles that just wouldn't cooperate. She dropped stitches and forgot yarnovers. She planned out the next project even as she was just beginning the current one. She abandoned some patterns and never started others.

She found creative solutions to problems and never looked back.

Whenever I see my grandmother, she seems to be fading more into the background. I don't know how much she understands about her illness, but she knows something is wrong. Where she once was a serial chatter and spreader of gossip, now she is content to sit and listen, watching the people and the world go on around her. Sometimes you can draw her out. By asking the right questions, she will talk a little about her children or her high school days. It's impossible to tell if she is remembering or just saying what she thinks you want to hear.

The next time I see Grandma, I'm going to bring my knitting. I'm simply going to sit with her. I won't demand her attention in order to soothe my guilt for not giving her enough of me in the past. There will be no stream of questions, no fishing for responses so I can pretend she is the same person she was five years ago. I'll accept her for who she is now, just as she always accepted me.

I won't try to undo my mistakes and regrets from years ago. I'll slap hot pink patches over the past and enjoy any future that we have together.

Notes on the Contributors

Katie Benedict was born in Hollywood, California, and lived in thirteen different states before her family finally settled in a small town in rural Alabama. She graduated from Birmingham-Southern College at the age of twenty, sporting degrees in both English and Theatre, and immediately headed North to figure out what she could do with them. Since then, she's lent her talents to a myriad of companies ranging from global financial institutions to a world-renowned Shakespearian theater. Katie enjoys way too many hobbies, including the obsessive reading of everything she can find; writing regularly on her webpage, http://oneschemeofhappiness.typepad.com/home/; and, of course, endless hours knitting with the girls at www.spidersknit.org, of which she was a founding member. She's quick to latch on to any opportunity to drag her friends to the theater for a movie or a play. Katie lives in Manhattan with her boyfriend and two very naughty cats.

Margaret Blank left full-time employment in financial services in 2004, after twenty-five years of writing retirement planning reports and money management articles. While a full-time caregiver for her ailing hubby, she tried her hand at writing, watercolour, and fibre arts. She credits her friends at the Alexandra Writers' Center in Calgary for the courage to make submissions. This is her first published personal essay.

Christy Breedlove lives in Georgia with her very patient husband, two active children, two cats, and two dogs. A former social worker of eleven years, she now is a stay-at-home mother who teaches knitting to elementary school students and still rides her mountain bike several times a week.

Barbara De Marco Barrett is a knitter, author, journalist, radio show host, and writing instructor in Southern California. She is also editor of *The ASJA Monthly*, the publication for the American Society of Journalists and Authors. Her award-winning book, *PEN ON FIRE: A Busy Woman's Guide to Igniting the Writer Within*, was a *Los Angeles Times* bestseller; her nonfiction has appeared in the *Los Angeles Times*, *The Writer*, *Poets and Writers*, *Writer's Digest*, *Pages*, and more. She is always thinking about knitting and has begun to create intarsia designs of her own. And because knitting is so often on her mind, she has begun to write about it, too. More at www.barbarademarcobarrett.com. Blog: http://knittingonfire.blogspot.com.

Donna Druchunas learned to knit before she could read. After working for twelve years as a technical writer, she decided to combine her interest in knitting with her skill at writing easy-to-follow instructions. She is the author of *The Knitted Rug: 21 Fantastic Designs* (Lark Books, 2004) and

Arctic Lace: Knitting Projects and Stories Inspired by Alaska's Native Knitters. Her designs and articles have been featured in *Family Circle Easy Knitting, Knitters, Interweave Knits, Creative Knitting*, and *INKnitters* magazines. Donna lives in the foothills of the Colorado Rocky Mountains with her husband, where she gardens and makes jam on the rare occasions when she doesn't have knitting needles in her hands.

Janet Engle continues to learn to knit from the turn-of-the-century cottage she shares with her husband and two sons. She is a freelance writer and edits the *International Data Rescue News*, a monthly publication that highlights efforts by government and private organizations to recover historical scientific records.

Alexandra Halpin is a native of San Francisco, the great-granddaughter of the first Lord Mayor of Baghdad, and, according to family legend, the descendant of a pope. She co-founded the Bay Area Wool Divas (BAWDies), a San Francisco knitting group. In 2004, she knit a sweater for Teva Durham's book *Loop-d-Loop* and has knit for designers Tina Whitmore of Knitwhits and Kristin Omdahl of StyledByKristin. She collects vintage patterns, particularly German lace designs, and writes about her knitting at www.oceanknitter.blogspot.com.

Amy Holman is a writer of poetry and prose, and a freelance literary consultant. Her final, sold book proposal materialized in 2006 as a guide to colonies, residencies, grants, fellowships, and graduate writing programs. She has a collection of poetry, *Wait For Me, I'm Gone*, published with Dream Horse Press, and many poems, stories, and essays published in print and online journals and anthologies. She also writes about knitting for *The Huffington Post*. Visit her at www.amyholman.com.

Hélène Magnússon was born in France in 1969. She completed a Master's degree in law and worked for a time as a lawyer in Paris. In 1995, she made a complete change and moved to Iceland where she began studying textile and fashion design. She has three daughters and now works as a freelance designer. Her privileged material is the unique Icelandic wool (www.istex.is), which appears in her work in various forms: knit, felt, or drawings of sheep. She seeks inspiration in old Icelandic floral–patterned knitted insoles used in sheep and fish–skin shoes in Iceland, which she develops in new and exciting ways. She is the author of the book *Icelandic Color Knitting: Rose Pattern Insert Knitting in a New Light (Rósaleppaprjón í n'yju Ijósi)*, which will be published in Engligh for the Scandanavian market by Salka (www.salkaforlag.is) and for the American market by Search Press (www.searchpress.com). More about her work at www.helenemagnusson.com

A native of rural Wisconsin, *Erica Pearson* now lives in New York City where she works for a major metropolitan daily newspaper. Since learning to knit two years ago, she rarely puts down the needles.

Dania Rajendra writes and knits in Manhattan, where she works as a union journalist. A New York native, she's done three stints in Minnesota, where hand-knit woolen goods kept her from frostbite. She fondly remembers her first hand-knit garments from Mom, who taught her to knit, and Ajji, her grandmother, who sent sweater vests all the way from balmy Southern India.

Born and educated in England, *Vera Vivante* emigrated to Canada in 1949. She studied ceramics and textiles for two years in Montreal and went on to design and make costumes for theatre and television in Montreal and Toronto. She established and directed an art studio, teaching ceramics, textiles, and creative knitting. She exhibited in four solo and several group shows. In later years, Vera pursued "creative knitting," developing a lace-effect, making lampshades, room dividers, window shades, etc. She has been teaching this art form in Quebec, Ontario, Upstate New York, and Georgia.

Sherri Wood is an interdisciplinary artist and improvisational quilt maker with a Master of Fine Art in Sculpture from Bard College and a Master of Theological Studies from Emory University. Most of her creative projects spring from her daily life experience. She often invites others into the art–making process as a way of sharing interior realities and exploring civic relationships that can lead to personal and social change. She has a private practice working with people in her studio who are grieving or in transition to make functional, improvisational quilts from the clothing of the deceased and the intimate materials of everyday life. Her best friend's mother taught her how to crochet when she was in seventh grade, and she learned how to knit "European style" from the mother of another one of her friends while in college. She is based out of San Francisco and Durham, North Carolina, and can be contacted through her website, www.passagequilts.com.

Detroit, Michigan (vicinity). Russian knitting bag and glass candle sticks, by Arthur S. Siegel, July 1942.

Credit: Library of Congress, Prints & Photographs Division, FSA/OWI Collection, reproduction #LC-USF34-110007-C DLC

Acknowledgments

I am grateful to the following people and places for their invaluable contributions to this book: Kari Cornell, Mary LaBarre & the MBI team; Clara Parkes; Linnea Anderson, Assistant Archivist, Social Welfare History Archives, University of Minnesota; Thomas Lannon, Manuscripts Specialist, New York Public Library; Patrizia Sione, Reference Archivist, and Barbara Morley, Media Curator, Kheel Center for Labor Management Documentation & Archives, Cornell University; Lucianne Lavin, Director of Research & Collections, Institute for American Indian Studies; Steve Grafe, National Cowboy Museum; Jennifer Lee, Rare Book & Manuscript Library, Columbia University; Larry J. Zimmerman, Public Scholar of Native American Representation; Faith Damon Davison, Archivist, The Mohegan Tribe; Dale Carson; Henry Street Settlement; National Museum of the American Indian; The Poeh Museum; Mitchell Museum; all the helpful archivists and researchers at the Library of Congress; Peter Constantine; Rob, ever-willing book schlepper; and everyone who contributed thoughts, research, and essays to this project.